Mammoth

from the inside

T0118157

The Honest Guide to MAMMOTH
and the EASTERN SIERRA

Colleen Dunn Bates

Prospect Park Publishing – California

Copyright © 2004, 2021 by Colleen Dunn Bates

All rights reserved. No part of this book may be repro-
duced or transmitted in any form or by any means, elec-
tronic or mechanical, including photocopying, recording,
or by any information storage and retrieval system, without
permission in writing from the publisher.

Published by Prospect Park Publishing
P.O. Box 91472
Pasadena, California 91109
www.insidemammoth.com

Special Sales
Bulk purchase (10+ copies) of *Mammoth From the Inside*
are available to companies, organizations, mail-order cata-
logs, institutions, and nonprofits at special discounts, and
large orders can be customized to suit individual needs.
For more information, go to www.insidemammoth.com

Printed in the United States of America

Design by DENTON DESIGN ASSOCIATES

Library of Congress Control Number: 2004096591

ISBN 0-9753939-0-1

Preserving the Eastern Sierra

Mindful that this book encourages and supports tourism in Mammoth and the Eastern Sierra, and that any increase in tourism can increase pressure to overdevelop the region, *Mammoth From the Inside* is a member of 1% For The Planet, an alliance of businesses committed to leveraging their resources to create a healthier planet. Members donate at least 1% of their annual net revenues to environmental organizations.

One percent of the net revenues (approximately ten percent of net profits) from *Mammoth From the Inside* will be donated to such Eastern Sierra environmental organizations as The Andrea Lawrence Institute for Mountains and Rivers (Alimar). Alimar is a nonprofit organization that seeks to establish a planning forum to identify key challenges confronting the Eastern Sierra Nevada, with the goal of preserving both healthy communities and healthy ecosystems.

For information on Alimar, go to www.alimar.org. To find out about 1% For The Planet, go to www.onepercentfortheplanet.org.

Contents

About **Mammoth From the Inside**

The restaurants, motels, condos and other businesses mentioned in this book were visited anonymously. No payment or favors were received from anyone, and this book is free of advertising.

Every effort was made to ensure the accuracy and timeliness of the information in these pages. However, businesses close every day, or change their hours, or raise their prices, or change ownership. Please don't blame me for this.

This is a personal selection of favorites. Occasionally I'll steer readers away from a place, but only if I feel that it is undeservedly well known; lesser-known places that weren't up to my snuff just don't get mentioned. However, I haven't been able to stay in every single cabin, hike every single trail, and eat in every single restaurant. So if I missed your favorite, please let me know:

Colleen Dunn Bates
Prospect Park Publishing
P.O. Box 91472
Pasadena, CA 91109
info@insidemammoth.com

Acknowledgments

First, my thanks go to Margi Denton, talented designer and enthusiastic cheerleader. I wouldn't have done this book without her. Thanks also to Margery Schwartz and Mel Malmberg, who brought their careful eyes to the manuscript when mine had grown too weary.

Thanks to fly fishermen Steve Terui, Dan Eisenberg and Kurt Ransohoff, the wise ones behind much of my fishing information. Tom McHenry, John Cook, Keith and Patti Dawley, Fred Richter and Chris Maese were a great help with camping, hiking and biking.

Thanks to my Mammoth buddies of the last decade. First and foremost, my beloved ski sisters: Sally Hackel, Sally Reeder, Patti Eisenberg, Janet Gillmore, Ceacy Thatcher and the late Lynn Angell. And the families who have joined my family in the mountains, making us all one big happy family: the Langs, the Cooks, Diane Park, Sean and Drew Dembowski, the Malmberg/Rohdes, the Ransohoffs, the Phleger/McHenrys, my brother Michael Dunn and his family, my sister Cathy French and her family, and, most of all, my sister Cammie Dunn and her kids, Kelly and Kevin Gould.

Back in the '70s, my parents, Joe and Ellie Dunn, paid attention when I came home from a high-school Mammoth trip raving about skiing, and they started taking our big family to learn to ski. They also told me I could be anything I wanted to be when I grew up. So now I get to be someone who skis, hikes, surfs and gets paid to write about what she loves. Thanks, Mom and Dad.

Thanks to Barbara Richter and Jimmy Kellett at the Mammoth Lakes Visitor's Bureau, Joani Lynch at Mammoth Mountain, Finn MacDonald at the Mammoth Ski Museum, Lynne Almeida at Spellbinder Books in Bishop, preservationist and ski legend Andrea Mead Lawrence, weather guru Howard Scheckter, the USGS map-makers and my Eastern Sierra book distributor, Marty Lewis, the multi-talented climber/author/publisher/bookstore owner.

Special snaps go to the Mammoth Forum folks, who've kept this city lurker going when she couldn't get to the mountains. Most of you don't know me, but you've all provided tons of advice and guidance. You can get to know them on Mammoth Mountain's website — click "Forum."

Adoration goes to my husband, Darryl Bates, who didn't bat an eye when I said I had a great idea to write and publish a book, which would then consume my entire being and a good hunk of our savings for the next year.

Finally, where would I be without my beautiful daughters, Erin and Emily? They've been my most constant Mammoth buddies, the two people I most love to ski with, hike with, sled with and hang in the hot tub with. This book's for you, girls.

INTRODUCTION

Doubly happy, however, is the man to whom lofty mountain tops are within reach, for the lights that shine there illumine all that lies below.
— John Muir, *Steep Trails*

In these few short pages you'll get started on getting to know Mammoth and the Eastern Sierra.

Falling **in love**
with the **Eastern Sierra**

It starts shortly after I pass through the sixth circle of hell, otherwise known as Mojave. As the airplane graveyard recedes, the desert spreads wide and the horizon becomes soothing, restful. Joshua trees appear, their arms reaching heavenward, or sometimes drooping downward. The joy begins to seep into my veins. Off to the west I spy the baby Sierra, modest brown hills hinting at what's to come. The joy meter creeps up a little.

I enter Red Rock State Park, driving Highway 14 past spectacular upthrusts of red, orange and pink earth. Getting pretty happy now. Soon I reach Inyokern, home to more Joshua trees. Those baby Sierras have grown into adolescents. Now I'm on Highway 395, and after a few dozen miles, the peaks are craggier, topped with snow. I drive on past Olancha and the vastness of the mostly dry Owens Lake bed to the east.

And then Lone Pine approaches. I'm having trouble keeping my eyes on the road, not to mention the speedometer. The full-grown Sierras now loom overhead, majestic and snow-covered and jaw-droppingly awesome. The joy meter is cranking full blast now. I've entered the Eastern Sierra, en route to Mammoth, and all is right with the world.

Over the years I've been lucky enough to have spent a whole lot of time in the magic zone between Lone Pine and Bridgeport. I've backpacked out of Lone Pine, camped out of Bishop, snowshoed in Inyo National Forest, boated on Gull Lake, hiked to Mammoth's many lakes, and skied the bejesus out of Mammoth and June mountains. Ever since my first high-school ski trip to Mammoth in 1973, I've been in love with the Eastern Sierra. And now that I'm a responsible middle-aged family woman, I've been doing my damnedest to ditch responsibility, pack up the kids and the skis or the camping gear, and spend as much time in the Eastern Sierra as possible.

My years as a journalist and travel writer, coupled with my many trips to Mammoth and environs, gradually led to a part-time job as an unofficial, unpaid travel agent for the area. For years I've planned regular trips for my family and groups of friends, and people are always calling me for advice. We have little kids and need ski-in, ski-out— where should we stay? Where's the best place near a lake in summer? Where can twelve of us go out for a nice dinner in Mammoth on Saturday night? Where should I rent snowboards? Is renting a Village condo worth the money? What's a fun hike that won't take more than two hours? How can we survive the Presidents Day crowds? Where's a good climbing school?

Eventually I realized how many people need help in planning a trip to Mammoth and the Eastern Sierra. Despite the zillions of dollars being poured into Mammoth by Intrawest (for better or worse), and the boom in visitors to the region, there's been no honest, practical, insider's guidebook.

Until now.

Colleen Dunn Bates
www.insidemammoth.com

The nuts **and bolts**

Let's start with geography. Where, exactly, is Mammoth located? And what exactly do I mean by "the Eastern Sierra"?

The Sierra Nevada mountain range runs for 400 miles up through the middle of California. The western side, easily accessible from San Francisco, Sacramento, Fresno and the coast, is better known; most visitors to Yosemite enter from the west, as do visitors to Sequoia National Forest and Lake Tahoe. The western flank of the Sierra Nevada is richly forested, with miles of oak-dotted foothills gradually giving way to pine forests and granite outcroppings.

The eastern side of the range looks like it's in an entirely different part of the world. Soaring, craggy peaks, most well above the tree line, plunge 6,000 feet or more to desert floors populated with Joshua trees, volcanic rock and, in spring, desert wildflowers. The landscapes are often awesome, with the sweep of desert on one side and the jagged, snow-topped peaks on the other.

Made internationally famous through the writings of 19th-century naturalist and author John Muir, the Eastern Sierra is a lot easier to get to than it was in Muir's day. Highway 395 runs along its base, connecting the towns that provide services for mountain visitors: from south to north, they are Olancha, Lone Pine, Independence, Big Pine, Bishop, Mammoth Lakes, June Lake, Lee Vining (where Highway 120 leads to Yosemite) and Bridgeport. The 395 continues north into Nevada, and it then accesses Lake Tahoe via Highway 50.

The tallest peak in the lower 48, 14,494-foot-high Mt. Whitney is one of the stars of the Eastern Sierra, attracting hikers and climbers from all over the world. But there's plenty more to climb besides Whitney, from the Palisade Glacier to the boulders of the Alabama Hills. Fishing also attracts lots of visitors; the streams and lakes of the Eastern Sierra provide some of the best fly-fishing in the United States. Lake-lovers of all kinds, whether they fish or not, consider this area a nirvana, because it has lakes by the score. And spectacular hiking trails, including the famed Pacific Crest Trail, zig-zag all over the place.

And then there are the winter sports: skiing and boarding at Mammoth and June mountains, snowshoeing throughout the vastness of the Inyo National Forest, cross-country skiing around Mammoth and up in the High Sierra at Rock Creek Lake, snowmobiling in huge, open meadows, and back-country mountaineering in the John Muir Wilderness.

Bishop is the commercial hub of the region and a favorite home of retirees and young climbers alike. But Mammoth serves as more of a hub for visitors, because of its beauty, its services (from condo rentals to ski rentals) and its proximity to everything from skiing to fishing, hiking to golf. This book, therefore, is focused on Mammoth, with plenty of forays into other parts of the region.

Finally, I know to be correct one is supposed to say "the Sierra," as in "We're going to the Sierra this summer." But no one really talks that way. This book is about the Eastern Sierra, but in its pages you'll learn about how to most enjoy time in the Sierras.

TEN THINGS YOU NEED TO KNOW ABOUT **VISITING MAMMOTH & THE EASTERN SIERRA**

Another glorious Sierra day in which one seems to be dissolved and absorbed and sent pulsing onward we know not where. Life seems neither long nor short, and we take no more heed to save time or make haste than do the trees or stars. This is true freedom, a good practical sort of immortality.

— John Muir, writing in *Atlantic Monthly*

When should you visit? What kind of weather should you expect? How do you get there? How can you find a babysitter? Do you need chains? How can you cope with the altitude? These questions, and more, are answered in this chapter.

Advance planning

It's lots of fun to spontaneously decide to dash off for a ski weekend, but if it's a holiday or prime-season weekend, forget about it, unless you like sleeping in your car in a blizzard. The motels, condos and even hostels in Mammoth and June often book up months in advance for Christmas week, Martin Luther King, Jr. weekend and Presidents Day, and on ordinary March weekends it's not unusual to find all the town's accommodations sold out weeks in advance.

A good location and a good bed will add much to your Sierra experience, so do yourself a favor and plan your trips as early as possible. And if you want to do any winter activities, especially ski/snow-board lessons, snowmobiling or dog sledding, book them early. Group and private lessons for Presidents Day weekend, for instance, are typically sold out six weeks in advance.

More visitors hit Mammoth in summer than in winter, so it's not surprising that the best cabin resorts are typically booked a full year in a advance for July and August. The better campgrounds that take reservations also go fast—you can make reservations seven months before your visit, and if you want a July or August weekend, you'd best be on the phone or website seven months in advance. If you have your heart set on spending a weekend at one of the non-reservable campgrounds, get there as early as possible to increase your chances of getting a spot (Wednesday is best!), and have a list of backup choices if your first choice is full. See the chapter called "Let's Go Camping" to find recommended ones, including some that accept reservations.

As for activities, if you hope to hire a fishing guide, go on a horse pack trip, take a rock-climbing class or go kayaking, book them as early as you can to avoid disappointment.

Altitude **adjustment**

The typical visitor to the Eastern Sierra drives in one day from roughly sea level to an elevation of 7,800 feet—and often within 24 hours, that same visitor puts on hiking boots, skis or a snowboard and goes up to 10,000 or 11,000 feet, sometimes more if they're racing up Mt. Whitney. Above 8,000 feet or so, air pressure decreases enough to significantly restrict the amount of oxygen molecules you breathe in, which is why that first hike or that first tramp up the stairs at Canyon Lodge can leave you gasping, even if you were fanatic in your gym visits in the months before. That drop in oxygen intake can also leave you feeling dizzy and nauseous; headaches are also common; and that shallower breathing often results in insomnia. The dehydration that results from the lower humidity at high altitudes can make many of these symptoms worse.

Solutions

Here are the most common ways to prevent and/or minimize altitude problems. Note that we're talking about the more minor problems, such as headache and nausea, not the more serious pulmonary edema or cerebral edema. Those are issues you need to take up with a doctor. Speaking of doctors, let me make one thing perfectly clear: I am not a doctor. The tips below do not come from a doctor. If you have any questions or concerns about altitude and health, please talk to a real live M.D.

→ **Hydrate.** Our family rule is that no one gets out of the car after the drive to Mammoth unless he or she has finished at least a 1.5-liter bottle of water. We also all wear Camelbaks (water-filled backpacks) while we ski or hike. Before we got savvy to the hydration solution, my oldest daughter got terrible stomachaches during every mountain trip. Turns out that what some experience as altitude-induced nausea manifested itself as stomach cramps with her. Once she started drinking lots of water, especially in the first 24 hours, she never got a stomachache again.

→ **Avoid alcohol the first night.** Okay, maybe one beer, but really, that's it. Alcohol is a depressive, and it further limits your body's oxygen absorption. Most people have adapted enough to enjoy festive beverages on the second night.

→ **Take it easy the first day.** Altitude-related complaints usually vanish within 72 hours, and for some, they're gone after just 24 hours. So if you're prone to altitude symptoms, start out slow. And if you're planning a Mt. Whitney ascent, don't even think about doing the one-day crash-course climb. See all those people throwing up on the side of the trail? They're the ones who didn't want to take the time to do it the three-day, gradual-acclimation way.

→ **Note the altitude.** My friend Michelle suffers from altitude-induced nausea, but finally she started paying attention to how high she could go. Chair 25 is fine, but on Chair 5, she turns green, at least for the first 48 hours of a trip. If you start feeling queasy or headachy, get down to a lower level. Sometimes descending just a few hundred feet can make a huge difference.

→ **Try Tylenol.** A Harvard study found that acetaminophen (the generic of Tylenol) and ibuprofen (the generic of Advil) are equally effective at relieving the symptoms of altitude-induced headache. But the study said that ibuprofen sometimes leads to gastrointestinal side effects, and it carries a small risk of high-altitude pulmonary edema. Acetaminophen is not known for these risks.

→ **Consider vitamin B12.** A number of people in my life stopped suffering from the altitude sickness that once plagued them when they started taking vitamin B12, an essential nutrient involved in the development of red blood cells. I've searched all the medical journals, and the only research I could find, pro or con, said that B12 can prevent the wheezing that is sometimes brought on from consuming sulfites (a common additive in wine and some foods). As I've said earlier, I'm not a doctor. All I know is that my husband used to get horrible headaches and nausea in the first 24 hours of our annual high-Sierra camping trip. My sister told him that she was saved by B12, so he tried it. He hasn't had altitude sickness since. Other friends have reported the same benefits. The word-of-mouth network says you're supposed to start taking it two days before you head upcountry. No need for megadoses—just an ordinary B12 supplement (or any B supplement that includes B12), maybe twice a day, has been enough to help the people I know. But let me just repeat: I am not a doctor. Don't take anything without asking your doctor.

Ugly UVs

The thinner air at high altitude also increases your risk of sunburn; if you're also on the snow or on a lake, that stronger sun will reflect and have an even more powerful effect. Basically, you're at risk of being fried, even on hazy days. Keep SPF 30 sunscreen on every part of your exposed body (don't forget the part in your hair!) and reapply at least every four hours. Finally, make sure to wear sunglasses or goggles with UV protection to prevent eye damage, which is a very real risk in the high Sierra.

Do I **really** need chains?

I can answer that question in one word: Yes.

But here are more words to explain. If you have a snow-loving four-wheel-drive car with mud and snow tires, like my trusty Subaru, you may never actually need to put on your chains. But if you visit Mammoth any time during snow season, you MUST carry them.

When snow and/or ice is on the ground, signs will be posted if chains are required. Here are the categories of chain controls:

→ **R-1:** Chains or snow tread tires required. Snow tires must have a tread depth of 6/32 inches with a "M&S" imprint on the sidewall.

→ **R-2:** Chains required on all vehicles except four-wheel drives or all-wheel drives with snow-tread tires on all four wheels. If you have four-wheel drive, engage it. Use the "4-high" range only. Use "4-low" only if your car gets stuck.

→ **R-3:** Chains required on all vehicles with no exceptions.

R-3 rarely happens, typically only when the roads close completely. However, you need to carry chains just in case. When the conditions get intense, the CHP will set up shop on Highway 203, and sometimes even on the 395, to check cars and order chains to be put on. In chain-necessitating conditions, you'll usually see guys by the side of the road who will put on your chains for a fee—which, ever since helping my father with a particularly disastrous chain-fitting episode in a Donner Pass blizzard in 1976, I consider to be money very well spent.

If your car is wearing chains, the speed limit drops to 25 to 30 miles per hour. Even if you have a four-wheel drive with snow tires, keep it to 25 or under when there's snow and ice on the road. Many's the time I've seen a four-wheel-drive SUV—sometimes even a more manageable Subaru—go slip-sliding all over a Mammoth street, sometimes right into a snowbank...or another car.

Fortunately, the town of Mammoth does an amazing job of road clearing during and after storms, so snow rarely lasts long on the streets. Black ice, however, is more pernicious, so keep it slow in town and on mountain roads throughout winter.

Eastern Sierra communities:
a primer

Here are the basics on the Eastern Sierra communities that attract visitors. Population figures are as of the 2000 census; for Mammoth (and probably Bishop), the number is certainly higher. The list goes south to north:

→ **Olancha.** *Pop. 134.* The southern portal into the Eastern Sierra. As tiny a town as you get hereabouts. Home to Crystal Geyser bottled water, the Ranch House restaurant and not much else.

→ **Lone Pine.** *Pop. 1,655.* Gateway to Mt. Whitney, the Alabama Hills, Manzanar and loads of backcountry adventures. A friendly little town with motels, coffee shops, restaurants, a Joseph's Bi-Rite market, gas stations, fishing stores and other essentials for outgoing or incoming back-packers, climbers and fishermen.

→ **Independence.** *Pop. 574.* The Inyo county seat, but don't expect a metropolis. Most notable for its grand courthouse, the curiously upscale (and wonderful) Still Life Café and the Eastern California Museum (760-878-0258), with fine exhibits on local history and an outstanding collection of Paiute and Shoshone artifacts.

→ **Big Pine.** *Pop. 1,350.* Gateway to the Ancient Bristlecone Pine Forest, Death Valley, Palisade Glacier, Big Pine Creek/Glacier Lodge and lots of good hiking, climbing, fishing and mountain biking. But lacking the charm of Lone Pine and Bishop, with fewer tourist services, such as restaurants and motels.

→ **Bishop.** *Pop. 3,575.* The commercial hub of the Eastern Sierra. Gateway to Bishop Creek and loads of Sierra hiking, climbing and fishing. A booming town that sometimes seems to be populated entirely with retirees and rock climbers. Some big-city perks (Vons, Smart & Final, auto repair) and lots of small-town charm (a great coffeehouse, a couple of galleries, a movie theater, an excellent bookstore). Good motels and restaurants.

→ **Tom's Place/Rock Creek.** *Pop. unknown (not many!).* A tiny hamlet just off the 395, with a motel, cabins, restaurant and general store. Ten miles up Rock Creek Road is the hamlet of Rock Creek Lake, with campgrounds, two cabin resorts, a general store, boat rentals and a pack station.

→ **Mammoth Lakes.** *Pop. 7,093.* The recreational hub of the Eastern Sierra. Nestled near the base of Mammoth Mountain and close to the fifteen lakes that the town is named for. Devoted to enjoying the mountains, with loads of ski and outdoors shops, rental condos, vacation homes, restaurants and recreational activities and services, from massage-therapy salons to ice-skating rinks, climbing walls to cross-country-ski trails.

→ **June Lake.** *Pop. 608.* The only real town on June Lake Loop, a.k.a. Highway 158, a fourteen-mile long bit of road off the 395 that's one of the most beautiful in the west, winding through pine forests past Grant, Silver, Gull and June lakes, with Sierra peaks looming overhead. A cute village with chalet-style cottages and motels, a couple of restaurants, a coffeehouse, a market and a few other services. Other businesses (cab-ins, restaurants, boat rentals) are scattered along the Loop.

→ **Lee Vining.** *Pop. 250.* The gateway to Yosemite, when Highway 120 is open in summer, and the town for wondrous Mono Lake. A few motels, eateries, coffee and gas; famous for both the first-rate Mono Basin Scenic Area Visitor Center and the gourmet Whoa Nellie Deli at the Tioga Gas Mart.

→ **Bridgeport.** *Pop. 794.* The Mono county seat. Known for its impressive courthouse and its small-town charm. Access to fishing and hiking galore. Not far from Tahoe.

Getting
there

At this writing, and for the foreseeable future, the Mammoth Airport is not hosting commercial flights. (The town and resort developer Intrawest are pushing hard to allow commercial jets to use the airport, to bring out-of-staters in to fill all those empty midweek rooms, but so far they haven't been able to pass environmental muster.) The only way to fly to Mammoth is to hire Gary Thompson, owner of **Mammoth Air Charter** (760-934-4279). He'll bring you from anywhere to Mammoth in his five-passenger Cessna T210—for a price, of course.

So unless you're splurging on a charter flight or flying into Reno and being bussed south to Mammoth with a tour group, you'll be heading to the Eastern Sierra by car...and there are worse fates than that.

If you're traveling from **San Diego County,** the fastest route is Interstate 15 north to Highway 395 north. You'll travel from urban freeway to the empty strangeness of the lower 395, between the I-15 juncture and Inyokern, and finally to the glory of the northern 395, with the majestic Sierra to the west and the Owens Valley and White Mountains to the east. (Be careful on the two-lane lower 395—it has seen far too many fatal accidents, and passing is risky business.) From San Diego, the drive to Mammoth typically takes six to six and a half hours, unless traffic is really bad on I-15.

Orange County residents can have the toughest drive, both because of the freeway congestion they must often battle and the difficulty in guessing which route is best. The shortest route is the 91 east to the 15 north to the 395. If you have the luxury of departing in the morning or midday, that's your best bet. But if you're leaving any-time after 3 p.m., forget it—the 91 can turn into a parking lot, and much of the lower 395 is a two-lane highway with dips that make for poor visibility. Passing the slow trucks often found on that road is hairy enough by day—it's downright terrifying at night. Instead, take the 605 north to the 210 west to the 5 north to the 14 north to the 395 north. You'll have carpool lanes on the 605 and 210, and once you get through

Pasadena, the sailing is usually clear. Orange County to Mammoth is typically six to seven hours, depending on traffic.

From **L.A. and Ventura counties,** get yourself to Highway 14 in whatever way works best from your home base. From the Pasadena/Glendale area, the drive is usually five hours; from the west-side it can take longer if traffic's an issue. Folks from Ventura and Santa Barbara usually need about six and a half hours.

If you live near **Reno,** or are flying into Reno and renting a car, the drive to Mammoth is about three hours, heading south on the 395. In summertime, you can reach the Eastern Sierra from **Yosemite** via a beautiful drive east on Highway 120, past Tuolumne Meadows and through Tioga Pass, but that road is closed in winter due to snow.

Just the stats,
Ma'am

Have you ever noticed how number-conscious many outdoors-people are? You know, the kind of skier who can check his altimeter watch at any given moment and tell you the number of vertical feet he's skied that day. Or the fisherman who can tell you the number of trout he's released this season. Or the mountain biker who counts the miles of single-track he's covered. (Funny that these number folks tend to be men.) Anyway, here's a bunch of numbers and statistics for those of you who like to know such things.

Elevation of Mammoth Mountain: 11,053 feet

Elevation of Mammoth Lakes town: 7,800 feet

Mammoth's vertical rise: 3,100 feet

Number of named trails at Mammoth: 150

Skiable acres at Mammoth: 3,500+

Annual Mammoth snowfall: 32 feet

Number of days of sunshine in Mammoth: 300

Elevation of Mt. Whitney: 14,496 feet

Elevation of Lincoln Mountain: 10,091 feet

Elevation of June Mountain: 10,135 feet

Skiable acres at June: 500+

Annual June snowfall: 21 feet

Number of lakes in Mammoth Lakes: 15

Number of lakes in Inyo National Forest: 400

Number of streams: 1,100

Miles of groomed snowmobile trails: 100

Number of campgrounds: 107

Year-round residents of Mammoth Lakes: 7,093 as of 2000

Peak seasonal residents: 35,000

Annual estimated visitors to Mammoth Lakes: 2.8 million

Number of those visitors who come in summer: 1.5 million

Annual visitors to Inyo National Forest: 5 million

Number of rental units in Mammoth: 8,500

Average length of visit to Mammoth: 4 nights

Average size of visiting party: 4.1 people

Miles to Los Angeles: 325

Miles to Pasadena: 311

Miles to San Diego: 400

Miles to Yosemite National Park: 32 (road closed in winter)

Miles to Yosemite Valley: 100 (road closed in winter)

Mother's little **helpers:**
babysitters & concierge services

Sometimes we all need a little help. From childcare to dinner delivery, reservation-making to hotel-finding, the folks below can make your trip to Mammoth an easier one.

The Adventure Agent
(866) 934-4882, (760) 934-4882
www.adventureagent.com

Sarah Calva's specialty is helping groups of ten or more have a great experience in Mammoth. She basically acts as a travel agent, with concierge services thrown in for free. So when she books your lodging, she gets a travel-agent's commission from the condo or hotel, and the cost to you is nothing. For no extra charge, she'll book your activities, from lift tickets and snowboard lessons to fly-fishing guides and climbing lessons. She'll also make your dinner reservations, charter you a bus, get you a babysitter and arrange anything else you need. The only time you pay her is if you need home delivery—grocery delivery and unpacking is $30 or 20% of the bill, whichever is greater. After eight years in Mammoth and lots of experience with local businesses and lodging, Calva is skilled at matching people with the right places and activities.

Doorstep Dinners
(760) 934-3463
www.doorstepdinners.com

Did you ski so hard that you can't even muster up the energy to go out to dinner, let alone cook? For $5.99 (plus a tip), Doorstep will deliver dinner from one of about a dozen Mammoth restaurants, including Angel's, Matsu, Whiskey Creek and two good pizza places, John's and Giovanni's.

Mammoth VIP Services
(800) 914-1333, (760) 934-8441
www.mammothvip.com

From reserving tee times to filling your condo's refrigerator, this concierge service does it all. They'll take care of your dog, get you a babysitter, make your dinner and activity reservations, plan your dinner party or your wedding, get you a massage, get your kid swimming or snowboard lessons, find you a good condo to rent—basically they'll take care of everything. When you arrive, your fire will be laid, wine will be chilled, reservations made and tickets waiting for you. For this you'll pay, of course: $100 to stock your kitchen, get the place ready and make your dinner and child- or pet-care reservations. To plan adventures, they charge $35 plus 10% of the cost of your first day's activities. Oh, and a personal assistant will run you $35 an hour.

Shaking 'n' baking:
quakes and volcanoes

One doesn't like to think about powerful earthquakes and lava-spewing volcanic eruptions when vacationing in a beautiful mountain landscape. But when that mountain land is the Eastern Sierra around the Long Valley Caldera, one needs to be just a wee bit aware.

The Long Valley Caldera is a geologic depression some ten miles wide and nineteen miles long, located south of Mono Lake and right near Mammoth. It was formed by a massive volcanic eruption 760,000 years ago, and today a volcanic chain still runs along the western side of the caldera, encompassing the Mammoth Lakes area. Other than when the snow level is really deep, anyone who skis or hikes just above McCoy Station will find a steaming sulfur vent, a stinky reminder that Mother Nature is still gurgling away underground. The last volcanic eruption was 250 years ago, which in geologic terms is about four seconds ago, and another eruption is entirely possible.

That said, there's no need to panic and go skiing in a fireproof suit. The U.S. Geological Services says the chance of a volcano erupting in this area is one in a few hundred in any given year. "This is comparable to the annual chance of a magnitude eight earthquake (like the great

1906 San Francisco earthquake) along the San Andreas Fault," reports the USGS website. If there is an eruption, it is likely to be small to moderate, beginning with steam explosions. There'd be enough time for people to safely evacuate.

As for earthquakes, they are frequent in the Mammoth area. (And thank goodness for that—there'd be no skiing if quakes hadn't made the montains.) In fact, as I write this, the USGS quake-monitoring web page reports that fourteen quakes happened in the Mammoth area within the last week. These were all tiny, unnoticed by residents, but happening nonetheless. Active faults run right through Mammoth, and it's just a matter of time until a large quake hits. That's when those of us who missed out on the recent massive real estate run-up may have a chance of affording a fixer-upper.

Earthquakes, however, can happen anywhere, anytime—even St. Louis, Missouri, is slated for a huge one someday—so don't worry about it. Just take note that the Mammoth Scenic Loop Road was not built to provide you and me with a pretty drive. It was built as a speedy escape route in case of an erupting volcano or large quake.

Weather

When Mammoth regulars are planning a trip, they say to each other, "What do the Dweebs say?" "The Dweebs" is short for Dr. Howard and the Dweebs, and no, it's not a campy rock band. Howard Sheckter isn't actually a doctor (he's a real estate broker), and he certainly doesn't look like a dweeb, but a dweeb he most definitely is—a weather dweeb, that is.

Since he was a little boy, Howard has been fascinated—actually, he uses the word "obsessed"—with tracking, understanding and forecasting weather. His obsession is Mammoth's gain—his website, MammothWeather.com, and his regular radio and cable-TV weather reports, are the most-relied-on forecasts in the area.

As Howard explains it, the regional forecasts put out by places like Weather.com represent too broad of an area. "Mono County is so diverse," he says. "You'd have to have two pages in a daily paper to do it right." So he focuses just on the Mammoth Lakes area, which has its own microclimate. It can be raining in Crowley Lake and sunny at Mammoth, or howlingly windy in Mammoth and calm just twenty miles away. Since he moved to Mammoth 25 years ago, Sheckter has devoted himself to understanding how climate works in the west, in the Sierra and in Mammoth. He started by drawing weather maps on a chalkboard in the ski shop where he worked as a bootfitter. As the years went on, and he studied the science more, he was asked to do weather for local radio and local cable TV. He started a free snow-and-weather phone, (760) 934-SNOW, which runs to this day, and his website is now linked to Mammoth Mountain's home page. Scheckter's "discussions" aren't always 100% intelligible to the non-dweeb—sometimes he gets carried away with words like "oscillations" and acronyms like "MJO"—but he always concludes his forecasts with a clear statement of what to expect...and in my experience, he is right most of the time.

In terms of the big-picture weather patterns in Mammoth, Scheckter says a lot depends on whether it's an El Nino year, a La Nina year or a neutral year. The 2003-2004 season was neutral, which meant occasional short, heavy storms interspersed with long periods of fairly mild weather. What 2004-2005 has in store is, at this writing, unknown. But in general, Mammoth gets about 300 days of sunshine a year, which means 65 days of snow/rain/clouds. The heaviest storms come between mid-December and mid-March, then snowfall tapers off pretty quickly. It's common to have 70-degree days in April and May, although early April can bring surprise dumps. Monsoon season is mid-July to mid-August—there's plenty of sun during that time, but thunderstorms pop up often, too. "The warmest, driest period is mid-June through mid-July," says Scheckter. "And the hottest time is mid-July, just before the monsoon season starts."

In September, the days are often in the 80s, but the nights start cooling, and by October, the nights are getting downright cold.

Regardless of the season, be prepared to experience some wind. "Winds are strong here because Mammoth sits at the very end of the Mammoth Pass, which is a natural wind funnel," says Scheckter. Regular skiers know that 60-mph gusts on the top are normal, and come summertime, the zephyr winds can get pretty brisk in the afternoons.

But in general, Mammoth and the Eastern Sierra are blessed with hundreds of days of temperate sunshine, lovely summers and just enough nice, fat winter storms to make its ski season one of the longest in the country.

When to visit

Mammoth has three peak periods: the heart of ski season, from Christmas through the beginning of April; the beginning of fishing season, at the end of April; and the summer holidays, particularly the 4th of July, the month of August and Labor Day weekend. The quietest times are in October and early November, as fishing season winds down, school is in session and the mountains are not yet open for skiing and boarding.

Avoiding crowds

In general, midweek is the best time to have the ski runs to yourself. There are two exceptions to that: the week between Christmas and New Year's, when the accommodations are always sold out, and the week after Presidents Day, which is a vacation period for many schools. Otherwise, there's nothing like an early-March Wednesday spent skiing or boarding Mammoth and June—just you and a few other lucky souls.

Problem is, most of us have jobs and/or kids and are consequently limited to weekends and holidays. If that's true for you, consider the Thanksgiving holidays and the weekends in early December, although be aware that the snow coverage can be spotty. A surprisingly good time to visit is the weekend before Christmas, typically the beginning of school vacations. Most people stay in the city, going to holiday parties and finishing their Christmas shopping, and after December 15th, the snow level is usually mounting, so this can be a great time for uncrowded hill action. Nothing will put you more in the holiday spirit than speeding down St. Anton with the family, caroling all the way.

Other weekends that tend to be quieter are the one in January before the Martin Luther King, Jr., holiday; the weekends in early and mid March; and the last couple of weekends in April, after all the Easter and spring-break holidays are finished, when the spring skiing is often fabulous.

The busy times
For thousands of Californians, spending the week between Christmas and New Year's at Mammoth or June is a tradition of many years' standing. For newcomers, the crowds can be a shock. If heavy weather moves in, as it did for Christmas 2003, much of the mountain can be closed for days, funneling all those skiers and boarders to the lower chairs, and lines can sometimes resemble the bad old ones of the late 1970s. Christmas regulars don't mind, and you might not, either, so long as you're prepared.

The other sold-out winter times are Martin Luther King, Jr. weekend in mid-January (sometimes the weekend after King is mysteriously crowded, too); Presidents Day weekend in February; and the week after Presidents Day, thanks to private-school "ski weeks." Because spring breaks vary so much from school to school, vacationers are spread out over several weeks in March and April, so bothersome crowds aren't usually an issue then. As for summer crowds, you'll find them on the 4th of July, during the Jazz Festival and Labor Day weekend. It's not hard to find a motel room in August, but the more attractively sited cabins and campgrounds book up very early.

For tips on how to make the most of the crowded holiday weekends, see "Holiday Hell...and Heaven" in Chapter 6.

Fall
There's nothing like fall in the Sierras: aspen trees turning golden, morning skies transitioning to a deeper blue, evenings becoming cold enough for a fire. And from mid-September until the opening day of Mammoth's ski season (usually in early November), the whole region is blessedly quiet. Snow can start in October, but often it's just a dusting, making this a fine season to enjoy quiet lake paddles, peaceful fishing

sessions and absolutely beautiful hikes. Just don't forget to bring a sweater and a rain (or snow!) jacket.

Spring
The calendar says spring begins on March 21st, but spring comes on its own terms in the Sierras. As I write this, in spring, it's 65 degrees in Mammoth, and the snow is melting so fast off roofs that the town is full of little waterfalls. But it would surprise no one if a monster storm barreled through in a week or two, bringing winter back again.

Fishing season begins the last Saturday in April, so for many, that's the first day of spring. For campers and hikers, it doesn't usually come until mid or late May, when the snow starts to disappear and some campgrounds and trails open. For skiers and boarders, spring appears whenever it's warm enough to leave the jacket in the condo and enjoy some corn snow.

The town and its rental accommodations are typically busy in early spring—late March through the first or second week or April, depending on when Easter falls—for the various school spring breaks. These vacations vary every year—many schools close the first week of April, but lots of colleges break earlier, and all the Catholic schools close the week after Easter. Opening weekend of fishing season can also fill up the condos and cabins. But in general, from mid-April until Memorial Day, things are mighty quiet...which is why this is often a favorite time for spring skiers and early-season outdoors folks.

As for weather, if you're in the Eastern Sierra in what the rest of the world calls spring—March 21st to June 20th—be prepared for anything, from a blizzard to a bikini session.

Summer
A cherished Mammoth saying is, "I came for the winter, and stayed for the summer." Skiers and boarders who can't imagine the place without a ten-foot base of snow find this hard to believe, but it's true. High temperatures average 75 to 80 degrees, and blue skies are plentiful. Meadow grasses ripple in the breeze, alpine lakes sparkle and, towering overhead, a few peaks still wear a coat of ice and snow. Hik-

ers, cyclists, kayakers, fishermen, climbers and golfers are in heaven from June through September. Rates at many condos and motels in Mammoth Lakes drop during the summer, making this a good-value season, although at the lake-area cabin resorts that thrive during summer, prices are usually higher.

If you're looking for summer seclusion, visit in June, when the town and the mountains are relatively unpopulated. The summer season is really just two months long: July and August. The crowd is more diverse than the ski-season crowd, who care only for snow sports. There are bus-tour groups en route to or from Yosemite; extended-family groups who've spent a week in the same cabin resort for 30 years; retirees doing driving tours; rugged outdoorspeople headed for, or returning from, the backcountry; avid mountain bikers eager to ride Mammoth's trails; and plenty of fishermen.

In general, summer weather is beautiful, with loads of sparkling sunshine and warm, but not hot, temperatures. But summer winds can blow, and thunderstorms can spring up with little warning, so don't set out for an adventure without a sweatshirt and a rain poncho.

Winter

Mammoth's winter season officially begins with the mountain's opening day, typically in the first or second week of November, depending on the snowfall. Opening day is a fun party, populated mostly with locals and diehard regulars who can't wait to put their season passes to good use, even if only six runs are open. Thanksgiving is the next rush, but it's still pretty quiet. Conditions on the mountain vary depending on how good the early snowfalls have been, but thanks to snowmaking, you can usually count on some fun downhill action, as well as sledding, skating and cross-country skiing. Many visitors during the early snow season aren't even skiers or boarders—they're just happy to breathe in the crisp mountain air and sit by a fireplace.

Winter may officially end on March 21st in the real world, but in this neck of the woods, it can go as late as April 30th. You can often ski and board into June—bring T-shirts and sunscreen!—but winter is considered over by then.

A GOOD
NIGHT'S SLEEP

The view was always fascinating, bewitching, entrancing. The eye was never tired of gazing, night or day, in calm or storm; it suffered but one grief, and that was that it could not look always, but must close sometimes in sleep.
— Mark Twain, *Roughing It*

Mammoth and the surrounding Sierra communities have just about every sort of lodging imaginable: cabins, cottages, motels, hotels, B&Bs, hostels, tiny studio condos in town and luxurious condos right on the ski slopes. The only thing missing is a five-star luxury hotel—and, like it or not, that's in the works. The pages that follow will guide you to the best home for your winter or summer stay, no matter what your budget. If you'd rather sleep under the stars, check Chapter 4, "Let's Go Camping."

The inns & outs

If you've ever tried to find a condo, cabin or hotel room in Mammoth before, you know what a confusing maze it is. Seemingly dozens of websites tout thousands of units, and before long your head is swimming in an overwhelming sea of information. Some say they're ski-in, ski-out, but does that mean a long cross-country trek through thick snow? The motels all sound good on the web, but which ones don't smell bad? And which ones are least likely to have an all-night party in the next room? Some condos boast that they're walking distance to the lifts, but does that mean a long uphill schlep...at the end of a tiring day with a crying 5-year-old weighed down ski boots?

My selection of accommodations is by no means comprehensive—no one could possibly review all 8,500 units in Mammoth, not to mention the places in June and in the mountains south of Mammoth. But whether you're looking for a luxury condo, a charming cabin or an affordable motel room, you'll find yourself a comfortable home below.

When to reserve

Know that you should book as early as possible, especially for winter weekends and year-round holidays, from 4th of July to Presidents Day. The better condos and motels are usually fully booked for Christmas week and Presidents Day several months in advance. Even ordinary ski-season weekends sell out in Mammoth. If you can't find a place in Mammoth during ski season, try June. If you strike out there, you might find room in Bishop (see the "Road Trip" chapter), but be prepared for a commute to the slopes.

If you're planning a summer visit, be warned that the better cabin resorts, especially in Rock Creek, Bishop Creek, Convict Lake, June Lake and the various Mammoth lakes, book up many months in advance. If you want a good lakeside cabin for a week in August, try to plan at least a full year in advance.

Midweek paradise

If there is any way that you can visit midweek, you'll pay much lower prices, and, of course, you'll have comparatively empty ski runs or hiking trails. My personal paradise is Mammoth on a sunny March weekday, just me, a few hundred other souls and 3,500 acres to ski.(Sadly, real life doesn't allow those days to come along often.)

Larger groups & houses

Large groups who don't know Mammoth well often search in vain for a nice big house to rent. What the city and Intrawest don't make clear to prospective visitors is that zoning laws forbid the renting of single-family homes in the town of Mammoth. There is a booming black-market business of second-home-owners renting to friends and acquaintances, but as with trying to get into show business, you have to know somebody. Because of this law, there's pretty much nothing in town that can legally handle groups larger than twelve. If you have a big group (as I often do), you may have to rent two or three condos next to each other—and while you can usually slip in an extra kid or two, resist the urge to put an extra half-dozen people on the floor—some condo developments have been known to kick renters out on the spot for violating a unit's occupancy limit.

Prices

At this writing, Mammoth's hotel tax is a whopping 12%, so add that on to whatever price you're quoted. (Tax rates vary outside of Mammoth; at Rock Creek Lake, for instance, it's 9%.) Also, almost every place in Mammoth charges 20 to 25% more for the week between Christmas and New Year's and for Presidents Day weekend; only some jack up the rates for Martin Luther King, Jr. weekend. Most motels and hotels offer some sort of AAA or AARP discount, so make sure to ask for it.

Also take note that this is an increasingly popular vacation destination, so know that unless you snag a bed at the Davison Street hostel, you won't be able to find a motel room, even a crummy one, in Mammoth for much less than $100 a night on winter weekends. If you're on a tight budget, try staying in June, Tom's Place or Bishop, where prices are a little lower.

Finally, be aware that prices can vary by season. Many condos and motels are substantially cheaper outside of ski season, but cabin resorts cost more in summer, when everyone wants to be by a lake. When the price varies by season, it is noted.

Condos **& cabins**

WORTH A SPLURGE

Double Eagle Resort & Spa
5587 Hwy. 158 (June Lake Loop), June Lake Loop
(877) 648-7004
www.doubleeagleresort.com

2-bedroom cabins $258-$319; packages available

The June Lake Loop is perhaps the most beautiful of all of the "developed" Eastern Sierra, and the relatively new Double Eagle has a drop-dead fabulous location right in the middle of it, on Reversed Creek at the base of majestic Carson Peak, in between June Lake and Silver Lake. The rustic-chic resort, spread leisurely over nearly fourteen acres, includes thirteen two-bedroom cabins, each of which sleep six and is quite posh (and expensive) by local cabin standards; a serious and full-service spa and fitness center; the beautiful (but culinarily disappointing) Eagle's Landing Restaurant; a fly-fishing shop and a trout pond, which becomes an ice-skating rink in winter. Owners Connie and Ron Black have created the sort of retreat that Mammoth is curiously lacking. The knotty-pine cabins are perfectly equipped with down comforters and flannel sheets, wood-burning fireplaces, full kitchens, barbecues, comfortable furniture and large decks. The place is known for its fly-fishing instruction, camps and guided outings; in winter, packages are offered for June skiers and snowboarders, and the spa has won national acclaim for its massage, seaweed wraps, facials, hydrotherapy and other indulgent treatments. The fitness center has everything from an indoor pool to yoga classes, and guided snowshoeing or summertime hikes are sometimes offered.

Eagle Run Townhomes

4000 Meridian Blvd., Mammoth
(760) 924-1102 (front desk), (800) MAMMOTH (reservations)
www.mammoth-mtn.com (click on "Plan Your Visit")

2- and 3-bedroom townhouses $259-$349 summer, $459-$725 winter

These fairly new townhouses are not exactly roomy, but they are well equipped and ideally located, especially for families—you really can ski in and out of these places, via the lower end of the Little Eagle chair, an easy beginner run. So you can ski little ones back for an afternoon nap, while more energetic family members keep skiing. Located just above the Juniper Springs Lodge, which has a coffeehouse, a little store, a swimming pool, spas, fitness center and other services, these units are tidy and compact, with good beds and all the conveniences. On a per-square-foot basis they're overpriced, but for some the Little Eagle convenience is worth every penny.

Juniper Springs Lodge & Sunstone

4000 Meridian Blvd., Mammoth
(760) 924-1102 (front desk), (800) MAMMOTH (reservations)
www.mammoth-mtn.com (click on "Plan Your Visit")

Studios $149 summer, $235-$310 winter
2-bedrooms $229-$289 summer, $399-$690 winter
3-bedrooms $329 summer, $510-$725 winter

These adjacent buildings, along with a tent-style lodge and a six-person high-speed chairlift, anchor the Little Eagle side of Mammoth Mountain. (In fact, this area is situated at the base of Lincoln Mountain, but that's a quibble.) Newly built a few years ago, these condos have proven to be a big success with families and couples who don't mind spending extra for slopeside convenience. What the units lack in space (and they do lack in space) they make up for in location: You really can ski to your door in many Sunstone units, and you can pretty much ski to the lobby door of the Juniper Springs Lodge.

All units in both buildings are kitchen-equipped condos, ranging from compact studios to three-bedroom, two-baths, which are also compact, but cleverly designed to fit in seating areas (some with little stone fireplaces), dining tables and, sometimes, sleeper sofas. You won't have room to spread out, but you do get all sorts of upscale-hotel-type amenities to compensate, including daily maid service, an inviting lobby lounge and use of the nice fitness center, pool, spas and game room. There's a coffeehouse on site, and neighboring Little Eagle Lodge has a restaurant, bar and ski rentals. All in all, for people who don't mind paying for it, Juniper Springs makes its guests happy.

The Village at Mammoth

100 Canyon Blvd., Mammoth
(760) 934-1982 (front desk), (800) MAMMOTH (reservations)
www.mammoth-mtn.com/plan/lodging/village

Studios and 1-bedrooms $169-$199 summer, $210-$395 winter
2- and 3-bedrooms $299-$359 summer, $440-$725 winter

Personally, I find the new Village to be a depressing example of the Disneyfication of Mammoth, and you won't find me staying there. But for many people, paying the premium is an investment in a relaxed, low-hassle vacation. The condos, done in a sort of mountain Craftsman style, combine the hotel-like conveniences of daily maid service and high-speed internet access with such upscale condo essentials as fireplaces, full kitchens and DVD players. On the ground floor are shops, bars and restaurants, including a Starbucks and a good bagel place. Handiest of all is the Mountain Center, where you can buy lift tickets, rent gear, book ski and snowboard lessons and hop on the new gondola, which will deliver you right on the snow in front of Canyon Lodge and its ski/snowboard school. The gondola is so quick and easy that you can easily pop back to your condo for lunch.

You need to know, however, that some guests have been most unhappy when they got units located too close to the bars, especially the ones near Fever, the nighttime disco within Dublin's pub. There's nothing quite like listening to the pounding of a dance beat at 1 a.m. after a hard day on the slopes. So make sure to book early and request a unit in a quiet area. Other downsides are a curious lack of storage—almost no drawer space for clothes, for instance—and a tendency toward overheating and stuffiness, so turn down the thermostat the minute you check in. Also know that the extra $85 to $130 is worth it to get a three-bedroom instead of a two-bedroom—the living and dining areas are almost twice as large, and you'll get your own washer and dryer (people in smaller units have access to a laundry room).

COMFORTABLE & CONVENIENT

The 1849 Condominiums
Lakeview Blvd., across from Canyon Lodge, Mammoth
(800) 421-1849, (760) 934-6501
www.1849condos.com

2-bedroom condos $160 summer, $340-$380 winter weekends
4-bedrooms $200 summer, $510 winter weekends
Substantial winter midweek discounts and winter holiday rate increases

Location is everything during ski season, and the 1849 has an ideal location right across from Canyon Lodge, a short downhill walk to the lifts—although parents of little ones take note that the walk home is uphill. If you want to be as close as possible to Canyon, request a unit in Phase One. A large, gray, fairly hulking building, the 1849 has two- and three-bedroom units in Phase One, with Phase Two adding some four-bedrooms. The units are roomy enough, and comfort levels are generally good, though the décor varies depending on the owner—I once stayed in one done in Early Viking, but I've seen others that are handsome and comfortable. Amenities include three hot tubs, an outdoor pool, a sauna, a rec room with video games, big-screen TV and ping pong, and a library of videos to borrow.

Big Rock Resort
Hwy. 158 (June Lake Loop), June Lake
(760) 648-7717, (800) 769-9831
www.junelakebigrock.com

1-bedroom cabins $125
2-bedrooms $150
3-bedrooms $225

This well-kept, ideally sited little cabin resort is so popular that July and August usually book up more than a year in advance. It's easy to see why. Although quiet and secluded, tucked into the pines on the shores of June Lake, it is convenient, too—June Lake Campground is next door, and the village, with its shops and cafes, is a five minute walk. The eight cabins (some of which are duplexes) share grassy lawns, lovely picnic areas, a friendly little shop, two small, sandy beaches and a private marina, with discounts for guests on fishing boats, pontoon boats, kayaks and pedal-boats. In winter it's all covered in a lovely blanket of snow, and June Mountain is just a few minutes away. The cabins are well equipped, with comfortable beds, kitchens, TV and VCRs, living rooms and outdoor barbecues. This is a fine home base for fishing, hiking, low-key boating, watching little kids play on the beach, and reading a good book in a chair under a tree.

Convict Lake Resort

Rte. 1, off Hwy. 395, just south of Mammoth Airport
(760) 934-3800, (800) 992-2260

Small, rustic cabins for 2-4 people $110-$190
More modern fireplace cabins for 5 $250-$310
Modernized cabins for 7-11 $215-$390
Very large houses $630-$995
Rates reduced for week-long stays; pets $15

A fisherman's heaven just two miles off the 395 and ten minutes from Mammoth, this cabin resort nestles below Convict Lake, about a five-minute walk away. The lake itself is a big wow: Sierra peaks, including imposing Mount Morrison, plunge seemingly straight down to the deep, blue lake, which is ringed with a fine hiking trail. This resort is best known for its restaurant, the finest in the Eastern Sierra, but its loyal regulars also have their favorite cabins. These range from the tiny and rustic—although all have kitchens, bathrooms and Direct TV—to the large and modern, with fireplaces, stereo systems and room for a big group. All of them have barbecues and decks. The cabins are pricier than at most other cabin resorts, but it may be worth it if your mountain idyll will be improved by the pleasures of a swell bar, a restaurant with superb $26 local trout, plentiful hot water in the showers, and easy access to dramatic Convict Lake. There's no boating, fishing or hiking in winter, but many of the cabins are available (the road is kept clear), making this a peaceful, snow-covered hideaway for skiers who don't mind the fifteen-minute drive into Mammoth.

If you can't stay here, make sure to come for a meal: Summertime lunch under the aspen trees is lovely, and wintertime dinner by the fireplace is even better.

See also the listings for Convict Lake Campground in the "Let's Go Camping" chapter, the Restaurant at Convict Lake in the "Best Food & Drink" chapter and the Convict Lake hike in "Twelve Great Hikes."

Interlaken

Hwy. 158, (June Lake Loop), June Lake
June Lake Properties Reservations
(800) 648-5863
www.10kvacationrentals.com/junelakepr

2-bedroom condos $175-$275 winter
3-bedrooms $280-$375 winter
July and August rates slightly higher

This small condo development has an excellent location on the shores of Gull Lake, a short drive to June Mountain and, in summer, near plenty of fishing, hiking and lake activities. The units are all spacious, but some are dated; if you want a three-bedroom, request unit 20—it has a view of the lake, fireplace, washer/dryer, granite countertops and good furnishings. Unit 30 is a particularly nice two-bedroom. The complex has tennis courts, spas and covered parking.

Mammoth Estates

221 Canyon Blvd., Mammoth
(760) 934-2884, (800) 228-2884
www.mammothestates.com

2-bedroom condos $120-$135 summer, $200-$210 winter
3-bedrooms $175 summer, $275 winter
4-bedrooms $200 summer, $330 winter
Presidents Day and Christmas rates higher; discounts for multi-night stays

Okay, so the construction is '70s crackerbox, and some of the units still boast harvest-gold "all-electric" kitchens. But you can't beat the value at this friendly, family-run place in the Canyon Lodge neighborhood. Unlike most Mammoth condos, which are rented through a myriad of agencies, all the units are rented through Mammoth Estate's front office, run by Thelma and Elliot Thompson, so you get an unusual level of personal service. The new Village is an easy walk in street shoes (not so great in ski boots), and three Blue Line shuttle stops surround the complex, connecting you to both the Village and Canyon Lodge. On-site extras include a swimming pool, a good outdoor covered spa, with adjacent sauna, showers, changing rooms and laundry room, and a game room with a pool table, ping pong and pinball. Units range from studios to four-bedrooms, and the price is the same whether the unit is a shabby relic or a spiffy renovation, so the remodeled places typically book up far, far in advance. If you want a four-bedroom, try to get 212, which boasts a swell new Ikea kitchen, handsome remodeled bathrooms, good beds and a massive TV/entertainment center.

By the way, Elliot Thompson is also a trombone player, and he and Thelma helped found the now hugely successful Mammoth Lakes Jazz Jubilee—you'll see him play with his band, Temple of Folly, every summer.

Rock Creek Lodge

Rock Creek Rd., 8 miles up from Tom's Place
(877) 935-4170
www.rockcreeklodge.com

Summer: rustic cabins $85-$95; small modern cabins $105-$115; large modern cabins
    $155; week-long stays discounted; pets $15
Winter: $95-$120 per person, including breakfast, dinner, transportation, trail passes
    and taxes

In the wintertime, when the roads up to Rock Creek Lake are closed, these friendly folks will pick you up on a snowmobile and bring you up to this rustic retreat at 10,000 feet, where you can cross-country ski or snowshoe for miles on fluffy, light snow. They groom fifteen miles of ski trails, and they'll even provide gear, guides and instruction. You'll be fed hot meals, have use of the Finnish sauna, and sleep in your own sleeping bag in a simple cabin heated by a wood-burning stove. For hardy cross-country and tele skiers, this place is a bit of heaven.

Less hardy folks come here in the summer and fall, to rent one of the cabins, which range from the extremely rustic (a cold-water sink only, meaning you'll walk to an outhouse and shower building) to the more modern and well equipped (if you want one of those, ask for one of the two-story ones facing the creek). You won't find a better setting than this: Rock Creek gurgles through the property, and the shimmering lake is a pleasant walk away, past meadows and aspen trees. The tiny restaurant, with two long family-style tables and a sunny deck, serves three meals a day in summer, and there's a general store for basic supplies. (Pretty little Pine Grove Campground is next door, so campers also make use of the store and restaurant.) Superb hiking, fishing and rock climbing are just outside your door; Rock Creek Pack Station, with horses available for backcountry trips, is a couple of miles up the road. No TVs, no phones—just mountains, lakes, trees, creeks and peace.

Sierra Park Villas

286 Old Mammoth Rd., Mammoth
(760) 934-4521, (800) 422-2644

1-bedroom/loft condos $95-$105 summer, $130-$170 winter, $200-$210 winter
*   holidays*
2-bedrooms/loft $125 summer, $160-$225 winter, $250 winter holidays

This middle-of-the-road condo development offers very good value for the money. It's located in the heart of Old Mammoth's commercial district, with a shuttle stop right out front and lots of restaurants, stores and movie theaters within walking distance; the location is great for families with teenagers (who want independence) or groups of friends sharing, who don't want to drive everywhere. Furnishings depend on the owner of the individual unit you rent; most are comfortable if a little frumpy. Units include one-bedrooms with one or two lofts or two-bedrooms with a loft and three bathrooms.

Snowcreek Resort

Old Mammoth Rd., Mammoth
(800) 544-6007
www.snowcreekresort.com

1-bedroom condos $135-$160 summer, $145-$210 winter
2-bedrooms/loft $230-$255 summer, $270-$400 winter
4-bedroom townhouse $365-$530 summer, $450-$775 winter
Discounts for non-holiday multi-night stays; discounts for spring and fall seasons

A sprawling, tastefully designed condominium community in Old Mammoth, Snowcreek has several phases, from the first clump of condos built in the '70s to the more recent (and fancier) townhouses. The quality of each individual condo depends on how well the owner has furnished and maintained it; on average, they're in very good shape. But the real selling point for Snowcreek is the amenities, which are considerable: renters have full access to the impressive health club (which includes childcare, yoga classes, racquetball and much more) and, in summer, the quality tennis facility. For guests, greens fees at Snowcreek Golf Course are just $18. Mammoth Creek runs through the property, which can be great fun for kids—feeding ducks in summer is a hit. In winter, the Red Line shuttle runs from the Snowcreek Athletic Club to the Village gondola, but if your condo is in the far reaches of the complex, you may have to drive to the slopes.

Tamarack Lodge

Lake Mary Rd., Mammoth
(760) 934-2442 (front desk), (800) MAMMOTH (reservations)
www.tamaracklodge.com

Studio and 1-bedroom cabins $125-$290
2- and 3-bedrooms $215-$360
Lodge double rooms $84-$110 with shared bath, $150-$185 with private bath

Dating back to 1924, the Tamarack Lodge is as charming as all get-out. Located on the shores of Twin Lakes, it comprises a central little lodge, a cross-country ski center and a collection of cabins scattered among the pines. Although the businesses of Mammoth are less than five-minute drive, Tamarack is blessed with a setting of Sierra beauty and seclusion. The cabins range from the small and rustic to the roomy and upscale; all of them have some sort of kitchen, and most have either a wood-burning stove, gas fireplace or wood-burning fireplace. They have good bedding, comfortable furniture and plenty of romantic charm. In winter, most cabins are snowbound, which makes them even more romantic.

In winter, you can cross-country ski, snowshoe and sled right from your door; in summer, you can hike and bike to many local lakes and canoe and fish on Twin Lakes or one of the lakes just up the road. The lodge's relatively small main room is particularly inviting in winter, when guests gather around the fireplace or at the game table next to the wood stove; a little snack bar serves everything from steaming French onion soup to breakfast burritos. The pricey French restaurant is a favorite of many locals for special-occasion dinners; even better is the summertime lunch on the little terrace overlooking Twin Lakes.

Timber Ridge

John Muir Rd., above Canyon Lodge, Mammoth
(760) 924-3991, (800) 262-8148
www.timber-ridge.com

1-bedroom/loft condos $110-$165 summer, $225-$325 winter, $295-$450 winter
*   holidays*
3-bedrooms/loft or 4-bedrooms $195-$250 summer, $395-$595 winter, $505-$725
*   winter holidays*

Built right onto the mountain, hidden in wooded slopes between the top of Chair 8 and the Little Eagle chair, these upscale, well-equipped condos truly are ski-in, ski-out. Diane, the rental agent, will give you accurate descriptions to help you choose the right place, or you can look on the website for detailed photos, descriptions and ski-in, ski-out details. Your location in the complex is important if some in your group are beginning skiers—from one end of the complex, you ski in and out from the easy Little Eagle chair, but from the other, you might have to negotiate some trees and part of the challenging Blue Jay run, above Canyon Lodge. Also, because they are located atop John Muir Road, getting up here can be tricky in stormy weather if you don't have four-wheel drive, though they make a yeoman's effort to keep the road cleared.

In general, Timber Ridge's condos are quiet and roomy—the two-bedroom, two-and-a-half bath is more than 1,200 square feet. They're not cheap, but they offer considerably more space for less money than Intrawest's ski-in, ski-out properties near the bottom of Little Eagle.

ON A BUDGET

June Lake Pines Cottages

Hwy. 158 (June Lake Loop), June Lake
(760) 648-7522, (800) 481-3637

1-bedroom cabins $75
2-bedrooms $85,
3-bedrooms $115
Holiday rates about 20% higher; pets allowed in summer for $5

These little chalet-style cottages aren't secluded in the woods, and you'll hear neighbors leaving for an early morning fishing trip. But they're a great value and are ideally located if you want to be in June Lake village. (I stayed here with teenagers, who loved that they could walk to the pizza place, the market, and the pedalboat rentals at Gull Lake.) Done in knotty pine, they ain't fancy but have everything you need: modest kitchens, sitting areas with TV and VCR, comfortable beds, little front porches and shared barbecue areas; a few have fireplaces. Request a cottage in the second row, off of Highway 158, and it'll be quieter; we were happy in #14, a two-bedroom that for $85 gave us a queen, two twins and a queen futon sofa.

Reverse Creek Lodge

Hwy. 158 (June Lake Loop), June Lake Loop
760) 648-7535, (800) 762-6440
www.reversecreeklodge.com

1-bedroom cabins $75
2-bedrooms $90-$140
4-bedrooms $285

The Naaden family runs this friendly complex of cabins, and they have plenty of workers to do the job: David and Denise have thirteen children, many of whom help out here. (And if anyone in your family has the same first and middle name as one of their kids, you get a five percent discount.) The plain but cozy one-bedroom cottages are a great deal for just $75, and the larger, knotty-pine A-frame cabins, perched above Reversed Creek, have killer views of Carson Peak; Chalet 16 has a particularly wonderful view. All the cabins have pillow-top beds, decks and barbecues, and many have fireplaces. June Mountain is about a mile away, and the town of June Lakes is a couple of miles.

SUMMER ONLY

Glacier Lodge

Glacier Lodge Rd. (Crocker Rd.), 10 miles up from Big Pine
(760) 938-2837
www.jewelofthesierra.com

Cabins $80-$95 for two, extra people $15-$18 per night; pets $15 per visit

Tucked alongside Big Pine Creek, with the mighty Palisade Glacier off in the distance, these cute little cabins are a very good value, especially because some can handle a decent-size group, and most have an adjacent tent pad, a good way to create an extra "bedroom" for kids. It's a quiet, friendly place, free of TVs and boom boxes; families play badminton, fish for trout, barbecue, and rent horses from Glacier Pack Train. The folks who own the place have a tiny kitchen in the general store, so if you don't feel like cooking, they'll fix you a hearty lunch (burgers, hot dogs) or dinner (steak, ribs) to eat on a picnic table or at your cabin. They can also set you up with a climbing or hiking guide—from this enviable location you can hike to Palisade Glacier, to various mountain lakes or along the John Muir Trail as far as your legs will take you.

Parcher's Resort

2100 S. Lake Rd., off Hwy. 168, 30 minutes west of Bishop
(760) 873-4177
www.bishopcreekresorts.com

1-bedroom cabins $110 for 2 people, $170 for four
Rustic no-kitchen cabins $90 for 2 people

The sister property to similar cabin resort Bishop Creek Lodge a couple of miles down the road, Parcher's has a better location along Bishop Creek, a little further off the road and closer to South Lake and the Bishop Pass trailhead. Also, it has the tiny, cheerful South Fork Restaurant, with a sunny wooden deck surrounded by potted flowers. The cabins are basic—larger ones have twin beds and a kitchen and dining area in the living room, as well as a queen in the bedroom, and the little, rustic ones don't have kitchens (though they do have outdoor barbecues) or extra beds. This isn't a fancy place; it's a simple but comfortable home base for those looking to fish, hike the amazing Bishop Pass Trail and listen to the sound of Bishop Creek and the wind ruffling the trees. Rates include a continental breakfast (pastry and coffee).

Rock Creek Lake Resort

Rock Creek Rd., 9 miles up from Tom's Place
(760) 935-4311
www.rockcreeklake.com

1-bedroom cabins $115
2-bedrooms $150-$180
3-bedrooms $275
Four-day minimum stay in summer; week-long stays discounted
No pets; open mid-May to mid-Oct.

I'm here to report that I have found paradise, and it's nine miles up Rock Creek Canyon, some 10,000 feet up in the Sierras. Lakes shimmer, aspens twitter, hikes and climbs beckon, fish jump, books beg to be read in shady spots, and a piece of fabulous pie awaits eating.

The King family has run this small resort since the '70s, and loyal fans return year after year for one of the peaceful, well-maintained cabins tucked into a shady glen. Gorgeous Rock Creek Lake, surrounded by aspens and lodgepole pines and overseen by Sierra peaks, is five-minute walk from the cabins; trailheads for some of the finest Eastern Sierra day hikes are a mile or so up the road. (See the Ruby Lake and Long Lake hikes in "Twelve Great Hikes.") Rock Creek Pack Station is also close by.

The general store/bar/café is famous throughout the Eastern Sierra for Sue King's homemade pies; on a sunny summer afternoon after a big morning hike, nothing beats sitting on the café's deck, having a piece of pie (perhaps preceded by a bowl of delicious soup or chili, washed down with a cold beer). At the store you can arrange to rent boats and get all the mountain basics, from trout flies to a bottle of red wine. The roomy cabins have good beds, good kitchens, decks and comfortable, TV-free sitting rooms.

Be warned: Families have been returning here for decades, so cabins book up to a year in advance. Start planning now!

Wildyrie Resort

Lake Mary Rd., Mammoth Lakes
(760) 934-2444
www.mammothweb.com/lodging/wildyrie

Lodge doubles $90-$95; cabins rented on a weekly basis only
1-bedroom cabins $784/week
2-bedrooms $1,043/week
4-bedrooms $1,694/week
Open early June to early Oct.

This old cabin resort had fallen into terrible disrepair, but then along came the Schotz family, who has owned Woods Lodge on Lake George for more than 50 years. They bought the place and spent a year fixing it up, and things are looking much better on Lake Mamie. Wildyrie comprises a small lodge with a few comfortable, inexpensive motel-style rooms, a collection of cabins and a wee boathouse, all scattered around the shores of Lake Mamie, one of the smaller of the Mammoth Lakes. Most of the cabins have lake views, and front decks to better enjoy that view. They're not fancy, but they're comfortable and equipped with kitchens, all linens and TV-less living rooms, and they're a good value. The town of Mammoth is a few miles away; from your cabin or lodge room you can walk to Lake George, Lake Mary, horseback riding and a number of excellent hiking trails. The boat rentals are reasonably priced.

Woods Lodge

On Lake George, off Lake Mary Rd., Mammoth
(760) 934-2261
www.mammothweb.com/lodging/woodslodge
Smaller cabins $595-$1,043/week
Larger cabins $1,155-$1,792/week
Open late May to mid-Oct.

Owned by Peg and Bob Schotz since 1950, Woods Lodge is a beloved cabin resort on Lake George that has seen families return for generations. There's no actual lodge with guest rooms, but the central office has a cozy sitting room with tons of books and games to borrow; outside is a comfortably furnished deck with spectacular lake views. Ranging from the small to the quite roomy, the cabins are folksy and comfortable, and most have wonderful views of Lake George and Crystal Crag. View lovers should request number 17 or 18, which almost seem to float over the lake. The better cabins book up very early, often a year in a advance.

Hotels, motels & hostels

WORTH A SPLURGE

Nothing! Rumor has it that a Four Seasons hotel is coming, like it or not...but for now, the luxury options are found under "Condos & Cabins."

```
COMFORTABLE & CONVENIENT
```

Austria Hof Lodge

Canyon Blvd., near Canyon Lodge, Mammoth
(760) 934-2764, (866) 662-6668
www.austriahof.com

Doubles $79-$99 summer, $160-$225 winter weekends (less midweek),
* $225-$315 winter holidays*
1-bedroom condo for up to 6 $99-$129 summer, $175-$315 winter

You can't beat the location of this small chalet-style hotel—at the end of the Canyon Lodge parking lot, an easy walk to the lifts. It has some of the quirky charm and comfort of a small, modestly priced European hotel. The down side is the risk of noise. Sometimes this place attracts loud guests who tend to come home from a night of drinking making a ruckus; then, if it snowed in the night, you'll awaken at 6 to the sound of heavy plow trucks clearing the parking lot and road for the morning rush. When the guests are polite and the roads are clear, however, the Austria Hof is a cozy little spot, especially if you score the king-bedded room with a fireplace and a down comforter. Extras include a small outdoor spa, a continental breakfast and a pleasant pub in the basement.

Holiday Inn Hotel & Suites

3236 Main St., Mammoth
(760) 924-1234, (866) 924-1234
www.holidayatmammoth.com

Doubles $132-$169 summer, $150-$200 winter, $227-$279 holidays

This place pitches itself as Mammoth's luxury hotel, and it is indeed pretty fancy for a motel—but deep down it's still a cookie-cutter Holiday Inn, with those motel hallways and polyester bedspreads. That said, the place has lots of bells and whistles: a sparkling clean indoor pool and spa, a small fitness room, a nice bar with a pool table and big-screen TV, and a good breakfast café. Besides the usual upscale-motel rooms (kings or double queens), take note of the king suite, which includes a kitchenette and a sofa bed, and the kids' suite, an oversize room with a bunk beds and an extra TV tucked into a nook. In-room amenities include refrigerators, microwaves, coffeemakers, HBO and high-speed internet access.

The Mammoth Creek Inn

663 Old Mammoth Rd., Mammoth
(760) 934-6162, (866) 466-7000
www.mammothlodges.com

Doubles $75-$85 spring-fall, $145-$185 winter
Suites (up to 4 people) $85-$95 spring-fall, $165-$295 winter

The former Jagerhof looks like the same old three-story, faux-Nordic chalet-motel on the outside, but things are looking way better on the inside. The new owners saw the need for a small, personal, full-service hotel—Mammoth had none, with the possible exception of the Mammoth Mountain Inn. The remodeled rooms now have excellent beds with down comforters and good cotton sheets. Even the smallest rooms have new, well-made furniture, including comfy chairs and handsome armoires. The larger suites have a couple of beds (usually a full and a queen) and a sleeper sofa in an inviting sitting area; a few have a kitchen instead of the second bed. Roomiest of all are the loft suites, which sleep six and have views of the mountain. The bathrooms are the old ones, so they're not as nice as the rooms, but they're clean and fine. Extras include concierge service, free ski/board storage, a game room/library, a sauna and hot tub, on-demand movies and games and a shuttle stop right in front. Located in Old Mammoth, just past the Minaret Center, the inn is planning a 78-room addition that will be pretty swank, including a full-service spa.

Mammoth Mountain Inn

Main Lodge, Mammoth
(760) 934-2581, (800) MAMMOTH

Hotel rooms $115-$175 summer (substantial discounts for MVP holders),
* $155-$340 winter*
1-bedroom condos $190 summer, $355-$420 winter
2-bedrooms $215 summer, $465-$525 winter
2-bedroom/loft (sleeps 10+) $245 summer, $690-$795 winter

There are more opinions out there about MMI than there are runs on the mountain. For my money, the condo units aren't worth the premium you pay for the ultra-convenient location at the foot of Chair 1. They're cramped and poorly equipped compared to most Mammoth condos. But the hotel rooms can be worth it for a short stay—only IF you get one of the remodeled ones. Some are old and dreary, with walls as thin as the April ice on Lake Mary, although ongoing renovations are gradually fixing all of them up. But some are quite comfortable motel rooms, with quality bedding and furniture, and at $175 for weekends, the standard rooms with two queen beds are not a bad deal, given the ski-to-your-door convenience—not to mention the ski bellhop and the other hotel services. The hotel's Mountainside Grill, its fancy place, is overpriced and too "continental" for down-home Mammoth, but the bar is appealing; the Yodler bar and pub, across the parking lot, is good for a beer and a simple lunch. Extras include an outdoor pool, indoor and outdoor hot tubs, a sand volleyball court (in summer), a coffee bar, a handsome stone lobby with a fireplace and comfy chairs, a video-game room and outdoor fun right outside your door, from skiing and snowmobiling in winter to mountain biking and hiking in summer.

Quality Inn

3537 Main St., Mammoth
(760) 934-5114, (800) 626-1900
www.meyercrest.com/qualityinnmammoth.html

Doubles $95-$189

Despite my dislike of generic motels and their polyester bedspreads (are cotton-covered duvets that expensive?), the Quality Inn is my favorite motel in town, offering a good value-to-comfort ratio. It's clean, it's quieter than most local motels, and the woman who maintains the breakfast area is a marvel of industry and cleanliness. That breakfast is partly what makes this place a good deal—you can fit up to four people in the two-queen rooms, and all four get the free continental breakfast, which includes good fresh fruit, yogurt, oatmeal, bagels and cereal. The huge spa is kept very hot, the parking is covered, a shuttle stop is out front, and the rooms come equipped with refrigerators, microwaves, coffeemakers and cable TV.

Rainbow Tarns Bed & Breakfast

Rainbow Tarns Rd., 1 mile north of Tom's Place
(888) 588-6269
www.rainbowtarns.com

Doubles $125–$155 summer, $110–$135 winter; no children under 12

Brock and Diane Thoman run a lovely and welcoming three-room B&B in a serene spot near Crowley Lake and Tom's Place. The inn's best part is the 1920s-era log-cabin wing, whose great room features an open, timbered ceiling, a big stone fireplace and comfy seating. Outside are three peaceful ponds; guests have been known to sit in one of the outdoor leather rocking chairs for hours, reading and enjoying the trees, ponds and ducks. The three bedrooms, all with private bath, are comfortable and well furnished, the breakfast is superb, and the house dog, Crowley, is a sweetheart.

Shilo Inn

2963 Main St., Mammoth
(760) 934-4500, (800) 222-2244
www.shiloinns.com/California/mammoth_lakes.html

Doubles $159 summer, $199 winter; higher on holiday weekends

This is where skiers with dogs stay—it's one of the better motels in town, and it welcomes bounding golden retrievers. The chain-hotel, cookie-cutter rooms are good-sized, with either a king or two queens and a microwave, refrigerator, coffeemaker and sink; rates include a decent continental breakfast and use of the indoor pool, spa and small fitness center. The Red Line shuttle stop is a short walk, as are many shops and restaurants. The winter-time ski packages can be a good deal.

Sierra Lodge

3540 Main St., Mammoth
(760) 934-8881, (800) 356-5711

Doubles $54-$119 spring and summer, $63-$149 fall and winter

A perfectly fine '70s-era motel offering a good comfort-to-value ratio. The large rooms come with mini-kitchens (fridge, sink, tiny microwave and dishes, but, curiously, no coffeemaker), small wooden balconies, a roomy area for ski boots and gear bags, basic furnishings and small, older TVs (with cable and Showtime). A basic continental breakfast is included. There's a pleasant little outdoor spa with a view of the mountains (and Main Street below), and a sort of rumpus room; games are available at the front desk. The lack of an elevator means you may have to hump your stuff up two flights of stairs, but that's a good way to get ready for the slopes anyway.

ON A BUDGET

Davison Street Guest House

19 Davison Rd., Mammoth
(760) 924-2188
www.mammoth-guest.com

Dorm beds $21.42 summer, $29.46-$34.82 winter
Rooms $45-$63 summer, $64-$100 winter

Carl and Maggy Hillenbrand run this friendly, hostel-style inn, where everyone shares the communal kitchen and sofa-filled, fireplace-warmed living room, and most share bathrooms. The house has two bunk rooms; the smaller, with two sets of bunks, is usually the women's dorm, and the larger, with five sets of bunks, is for men—but if you book for a group of women, you'll get the larger bunk room. At these prices, you're expected to clean up after yourself, which most guests are good about. This place is a godsend for skiers and hikers on a budget—but it books up early.

June Lake Villager Motel

Hwy. 158 (June Lake Loop), June Lake
(760) 648-7712, (800) 655-6545
www.junelakevillager.com

Doubles $50-$75
Cabins/suites $75-$195
Holiday rates may be higher; pets welcome

Although nothing fancy, the knotty-pine motel rooms are a swell deal here. The queen-bed doubles are as cheap as $50 midweek in ski season. The place is pet-friendly, and new owners are looking to spiff up a bit, adding continental breakfast and afternoon tea. The larger cabins and housekeeping suites have full kitchens.

Motel 6

3272 Main St., Mammoth
(760) 934-6660, (888) 466-8356

Doubles $52-$72 summer, $62-$86 winter

Everyone knows what the Motel 6 is all about: generic, no-frills motel rooms. No breakfast, no refrigerator, no nothing. It's one of the cheapest motels in town, but at nearly $100 (including tax) for winter weekends, it's not exactly cheap, and you don't get much for the money. There's also a risk of loud partiers in the wee hours. I'd rather spend a few bucks more for a place with a little more personality, or really go budget and stay at the Davison Street hostel. But this is a handy place to know about if everything is booked.

Tom's Place Resort

Off Hwy. 395, Tom's Place
(760) 935-4239
www.tomsplaceresort.com

Dorm-room beds $20
Lodge doubles $45-$55
Cabins $60-$100

Long a way station for Eastern Sierra travelers, Tom's Place is a winningly funky vacation complex found just off the 395. It's not in a mountain wilderness, but the folks here don't mind—not only is Tom's Place cheap, but great fishing on Crowley Lake is moments away, Rock Creek Lake is nine miles up the mountain, and Mammoth's skiing is about twenty-minute drive. The complex includes a general store, a large café and bar (where grizzled locals hold court), a few basic cabins, a lodge with modest bed-rooms (bathrooms down the hall) and a small dormitory, where you can have a clean bed for just $20. When the town of Mammoth is full, or too pricey, it might be worth a commute to Tom's Place.

4

LET'S GO
CAMPING!

You may be a little cold some nights, on mountain tops above the timber-line, but you will see the stars, and by and by you can sleep enough in your town bed, or at least in your grave.

—John Muir, *Our National Parks*

The Eastern Sierra is positively thick with public campgrounds, some with room for just a few tents, others that can accommodate big RVs. Of the dozens and dozens of campgrounds, here are my favorites.

The camper's
helper

This was a challenging chapter to keep to a reasonable size. Camping is just one part of experiencing the Eastern Sierra, so I had to limit the campgrounds to a moderate number—but winnowing down the list wasn't easy. The region is full of lovely campgrounds: nestled next to lakes, alongside creeks, or in shady forests. In the pages that follow you'll find my favorite Eastern Sierra campgrounds; the majority are in the Mammoth area, but they also include such heavenly locations as Big Pine Creek, Rock Creek Lake and June Lake. Most have at least some reservable sites, but a few—notably the ones in the Devil's Postpile/Red's Meadow area and around the Mammoth lakes—do not. This can be a good thing—those hoping for a last-minute trip have a better shot at getting a good campsite.

All of these campgrounds are closed in the snow seasons. Spring/summer openings depend on the elevation and typical snow-pack. Most shut down by early October, but a few go until November. In late spring and fall, you're more likely to be able to show up at any of these campgrounds and find a good spot (fall is a particularly quiet and beautiful time in the Sierras). In summer, most fill up fast. If the campground you want accepts reservations, make them as early as possible. And if you want to try your luck for one that doesn't take reservations, show up midweek, cross your fingers and have a list of backup sites.

Also, if you're planning on arriving on either end of a campground's season, call first to make sure it will actually be open—weather and snow can change opening and closing dates.

Remember, all of these campgrounds are in bear country, and the bears of the Eastern Sierra have become more numerous and aggressive in recent years. They want your food (not you!), and if you give them any reason to think they can get at your food, they'll wreck coolers and even cars trying to get at it. So every campsite is equipped with a bear-proof locker. And you need to use it. Do not leave ANY food out, or in your car, or in a cooler under the picnic table. You will regret it!

Finally, I will confess to a small bias toward tent camping over RV camping—to me, spending time in nature means time away from generators, electric lights and such. You may sense that bias in the reviews that follow. But most of these campgrounds welcome RVs, and I have no doubt that every RVer reading this book is a sensitive sort who respects the peaceful natural setting of a Sierra campground.

Bishop
& environs

Big Pine Creek
Big Pine Creek
Up Glacier Lodge Rd. (Crocker Rd.), 10 miles west of Big Pine
(760) 873-2500

Reservations: (877) 444-6777, www.reserveamerica.com
Open May-mid-Oct.; 12 tent sites, 24 tent/RV sites (36-ft. limit); water, chemical toilets,
tables, barbecues, fire rings, pets; showers at Glacier Lodge

Big Pine Creek rushes alongside this small, exceptionally beautiful National Forest campground, part of the Glacier Lodge complex. The old lodge burned down several years ago, but a number of services are still offered, including a tiny general store that will make you a steak dinner, a little stocked trout pond that's great for kids, and a pack station just down the road, where you can rent horses for an hour's ride or book an overnight pack trip. The surroundings are superb—you can take a short, easy hike to First Falls; longer hikes to Second Falls, Lon Chaney's old cabin and several lovely lakes; or a serious climbing trip to Palisade Glacier, which you can see from the campground. The coolest campsite is number 9, a tent site that includes a massive old stone fireplace, a remnant from the old Glacier Lodge days.

East Fork

Rock Creek Rd., 6 miles south of Tom's Place, Rock Creek Lake
(760) 873-2500

Reservations: (877) 444-6777, www.reserveamerica.com
Open May-Oct.; 53 tent sites, 80 tent/RV sites (36-ft. RV limit); water, flush toilets,
*   tables, barbecues, fire rings, pets*

This is the closest campground with reservable sites near spectacular Rock Creek Lake and Mosquito Flat; Rock Creek Lake and Pine Grove are better located and prettier, but neither accepts reservations. At a 9,000-foot elevation in Little Lakes Canyon, a few miles south of Rock Creek Lake, the 133 campsites cluster along rushing Rock Creek. Because the sites along the creek are larger, that's where the RVs go; in the busy season, tent campers seeking privacy choose the smaller, more secluded sites away from the creek. (Sites 121 to 123 have nice pine-tree shade.) A trail from the campground leads three miles or so to Rock Creek Lake; from there you can find your way to the store/café at Rock Creek Lake Resort, where you can feast on Sue King's pies.

Onion Valley

Onion Valley Rd., 13 miles west of Independence
(760) 876-6200

Reservations: (877) 444-6777, www.reserveamerica.com
Open June-Sept.; 17 tent sites, 12 tent/RV sites (28-ft. RV limit); water, flush toilets,
*   tables, barbecues, fire rings, pets*

Because of its high altitude (9,200 feet) and therefore heavy winter snow-pack, the camping season is short at Onion Valley. And thanks to the campground's small size and bucolic setting in between Robinson and Independence creeks, it is extremely popular—so don't show up without a reservation. This is first-rate summer wildflower country, and the hikes up along either creek lead to gorgeous lakes, flowers and peaks.

Rock Creek Lake

Rock Creek Rd., 9 miles south of Tom's Place
(760) 873-2500

No reservations
Open May-Nov.; 28 sites (32-ft. RV limit); water, flush toilets, tables, barbecues, fire
*   rings, pets*

Lovely campsites are tucked among the trees along the far shore of shimmering Rock Creek Lake, beloved for its fishing and its wonderful hiking trails. Good rock climbing and horseback riding are also found hereabouts, and the friendly general store, with boat rentals, supplies and famous homemade pies, is an easy walk away. The balance is more tents than RVs, and the overall atmosphere is quiet and peaceful. Some sites are a little too close together; tent campers seeking more privacy should request sites 20 to 24. Unfortunately, all the sites are now for walk-ins only, so you take your chances in July and August—this high-altitude heaven always seems full. (If it is full and you strike out, work your way downhill on Rock Creek Road to the other campgrounds: Pine Grove, East Fork, Palisade, Big Meadow and Iris.) You'll find something eventually. Rock Creek Lake's more exposed group campsite, which can handle up to 25 people, is reservable; call (877) 444-6777, or go towww.reserveamerica.com.

Mammoth
& environs

Convict Lake

Up Convict Lake Rd., 2 miles west of Hwy. 395, between Crowley Lake and Mammoth
(760) 924-5500

No reservations
Open April-Oct.; 88 sites (50-ft. RV limit); water, flush toilets, tables, barbecues, fire
*   rings, pets; showers at Convict Lake Resort*

I could do with a few less RVs, a little more shade and a few less beer cans in Convict Creek, but nonetheless this is a campground worth knowing about. It's a particular find in spring, when many higher-elevation campgrounds haven't opened yet. The crowds haven't moved in yet, so you can camp in peace, drive fifteen minutes to Mammoth to ski in the morning, and come back here to hike, fish or canoe in the afternoon. This campground is one of the most popular in the Eastern Sierra, with 94% average occupancy, so during the peak season, be prepared for lots of people. Early birds get the few shady sites under the trees; most are exposed. Just across the creek is Convict Lake Resort, with a good general store and a first-rate fancy restaurant.

Lake George

Off Lake Mary Rd., 5 miles southwest of Mammoth
(760) 924-5500

No reservations
Open June-Sept.; 16 sites (20-ft. RV limit); water, flush toilets, tables, barbecues, fire rings, pets; showers at Twin Lakes store or Lake Mary Marina

With just sixteen sites, this family-favorite campground fills up fast in summertime. It's located on a small rise above Lake George (some of the sites have fine lake views), which means it can get pretty breezy when the afternoon Sierra winds start blowing. But that's a small price to pay for the access to tree-lined, trout-stocked Lake George (and its little boat-renting marina), neighboring Lake Mary and Lake Mamie, and many fine trails, including those to T.J. Lake and Emerald Lake.

Minaret Falls

Off Minaret Summit Rd. (Hwy. 203), 12 miles west of Mammoth
(760) 924-5500

No reservations
Open June-Oct.; 27 sites (36-ft. RV limit); water, flush toilets, tables, barbecues, fire rings, pets allowed

Because it is located one mile down a dirt road off Highway 203, this is the quietest campground in the San Joaquin River valley, removed from the grinding gears of the shuttle buses running up and down every day in summer. It's also one of the loveliest campgrounds in the whole region. Only 27 well-spaced sites are nestled in pines and aspens along the eastern shore of the San Joaquin; on a lazy afternoon, the only sounds you hear are the water and the birds. Although you can hear Minaret Falls from this campground, you can't easily access them, because they're on the other side of the San Joaquin. So are the Pacific Crest and John Muir trails; to reach them, follow the east-shore trail a mile or so down toward Devil's Postpile to cross the bridge. Trout-rich Sotcher Lake and the store and café at Red's Meadow are easy hikes away (about two level miles to Sotcher and three to Red's Meadow). Because of its beauty and location, these sites are always full; your only hope of scoring a site (outside of sheer luck) is to arrive midweek. Fall is gorgeous and an easier time to get a site.

New Shady Rest & Old Shady Rest

Sawmill Rd., off Hwy. 203 (Main St.), Mammoth
(760) 924-5500

Reservations: (877) 444-6777, www.reserveamerica.com
Open May-Oct.; 94 sites (55-ft. RV limit); water, flush toilets, tables, barbecues, fire
*   rings, pets; showers at Mammoth Mountain RV Park across Main St.*

You can almost always find a shady spot to camp under the towering pines here at the New Shady Rest, or at its sister campground next door, Old Shady Rest. That's because it's right on the edge of Mammoth town, not in a pristine Sierra wilderness. But nonetheless it's a swell place to camp, particularly if you want easy access to such town amenities as stores and restaurants. From here cyclists can hook into lots of mountain and road routes, and all sorts of trailheads, fishing spots, hot springs and activities.

Red's Meadow

Off Minaret Summit Rd. (Hwy. 203), 14 miles southwest of Mammoth
(760) 924-5500

No reservations
Open June-Sept.; 56 sites (50-ft. RV limit); water, flush toilets, tables, barbecues, fire
*   rings, pets; free mineral-springs showers on site*

A wonderful campground along the San Joaquin River, near Devil's Postpile, the Pacific Crest Trail and the John Muir Trail, this place is probably most famous for its free showers, which are fed by the natural hot springs burbling underground. Nothing feels better after an all-day hike than one of those mineral-water showers. Reservations aren't taken, and this place fills up fast, so trying midweek is your best bet. Red's Meadow Resort, with its restaurant, cabins, general store and pack station, is an easy walk, and the fishing and hiking are world-class.

Sherwin Creek

On Sherwin Creek Rd. (dirt road), off Old Mammoth Rd., Mammoth
(760) 924-5500

Reservations: (877) 444-6777
Open June-Sept.; 87 sites (50-ft. RV limit); water, pit toilets, tables, barbecues, fire rings,
*   pets; showers at Whitmore Pool (760-935-4222)*

This campground in the shade of a tall-pine forest is so peaceful and quiet, it's hard to imagine that the bustling town of Mammoth is just a mile or so away. The quiet is due to the relative remoteness of Sherwin Creek—it is reached only by a rutted dirt road, one end of which empties out onto the 395 a couple of miles south of the main Mammoth exit, the other end of which is found on Old Mammoth Road, just beyond all the businesses. Even though this is a large campground that allows large RVs, it's roomy enough to allow for plenty of privacy; tent campers will like the quiet at walk-in sites 1 to 15. Site 60 is also a good one, a large, private spot with views of the surrounding hillsides. Trout-stocked Sherwin Creek runs through the campground, and the trailheads for Sherwin and Valentine lakes are close by.

Twin Lakes

Twin Lakes turnoff off Lake Mary Rd., 3 miles southwest of Mammoth
(760) 924-5500

No reservations
Open May-Nov.; 95 sites (50-ft. RV limit); water, flush toilets, tables, barbecues, fire
*   rings, pets; showers at general store*

Families return year after year to this large campground set in the shade of tall pines along the shores of Twin Lakes. People bring their bikes, fishing poles, kayaks, canoes, hiking boots, camp chairs and summer reading, and use them all. The classic old tin-roofed Twin Lakes Store sells everything from bait to marshmallows to showers, and it also rents boats. A short walk up the road is Tamarack Lodge, with its fine, upscale restaurant. The campground doesn't take reservations, but it's large enough to handle a crowd, so your chances are better here than at, say, Lake George or Minaret Falls.

June Lake
loop

June Lake

Off Hwy. 158 (June Lake Loop), June Lake
(760) 647-3045

Reservations: (877) 444-6777 , www.reserveamerica.com
Open April–Nov.; 28 sites (32-ft. RV limit); water, flush toilets, tables, barbecues, fire
*   rings, pets allowed*

The June Lake Loop has several fine campgrounds; this one is ideal for families, people who want easy boating access and those who'd like to be able to walk to town. It's small, with just 28 sites, so reserve early if you hope to get a spot (a few of the best sites, closest to the lake, are saved for walk-ins, and they go fast). The campground has sites on the southeast shore of June Lake, in between Big Rock Resort and the June Lake Marina, both of which rent boats (kayaks, pedalboats, fishing boats, pontoon boats). The town shops and cafes are a five-minute walk.

Oh! Ridge

Off Hwy. 158 (June Lake Loop), June Lake
(760) 647-3045

Reservations: (877) 444-6777, www.reserveamerica.com
Open April–Nov.; 148 sites (40-ft. RV limit); water, flush toilets, tables, barbecues, fire
*   rings, showers at neighboring Pine Cliff resort*

If you want to be in the June area and prefer a campground with a little more privacy and room to roam than June Lake Campground, head for the larger Oh! Ridge on the northeast side of the lake. Town shops and boat rentals aren't walking distance, but June's two swimming beaches are. (June is the best lake in the area for swimming.) And then there's the view: You're likely to exclaim "Oh!" when you wake up in the morning to see the sun illuminating June Mountain and Carson Peak towering over June Lake. The RV-clogged Pine Cliff Resort is next door, so there's convenient access to showers and a general store.

THE BEST
FOOD & DRINK

The best bill of fare I know of is a good appetite.
—Josh Billings, *His Works Complete*

Let's get out of those wet clothes and into a dry martini.
—Robert Benchley

Working up an appetite— and a thirst—is never a problem in Mammoth and the Eastern Sierra. In the pages that follow, you'll find just the right place to quell both your appetite and your thirst, whether you're seeking a short stack or a sesame-seared ahi, a Perrier or a Pinot Noir, a decaf coffee or a double-shot latte. Bon appetit!

Gourmet
paradise?

Mammoth may be a major tourist destination, but it's still a small town, and June, Bishop and Lone Pine are even smaller...and people don't move to the small towns of the Eastern Sierra for the food. So don't go into the area expecting to find lots of the chic bistros, authentic ethnic joints and upscale culinary showcases that are plentiful in places like Santa Monica, Santa Barbara and San Diego.

That said, there's plenty of good eating in the Eastern Sierra, as long as your expectations are reasonable and your appetite is good—which is highly likely if you've spent your day skiing, boarding, hiking, climbing or otherwise living the mountain life. Be prepared to pay a little more than you would at home—this is a tourist destination, after all—and don't get too hung up on big-city standards, and you'll find plenty of good food and drink.

About prices

Price ranges for restaurants aren't given, because they vary so greatly depending on what you order. The breakfast and coffee places are usually less than $10 a head. The happy-hour and pub food often hovers around the $10-per-entrée mark. "Mid-Range" restaurants are everyday, informal places, where a main course for dinner might run, say, $8 for a burger or $15 to $20 for a fancier entrée. "Upscale" places are more for special occasions, or for people who are used to higher-end dining and don't mind spending for it. At these places, you're likely to pay from $20 to $30 for a main course.

About hours

Because this is a resort region with wildly fluctuating numbers of visitors, very few restaurants or bars like to say when closing time is. If it's a dead night, they might close up shop at 8, even if they say they close at 9. Conversely, they're not about to turn away business, so they may stay open until 10:30. So you are well advised to call before showing up on the late side at any Mammoth restaurant.

In general, this is an early-bird town. People are hungry from a day outdoors, so they're lining up to eat by 6. By 9, many restaurants are deserted.

A LIST OF **BEST BETS**

Here are my personal favorites:

- *Best all-around restaurant:* Nevados
- *Best breakfast:* Blondie's
- *Best coffeehouse:* The Looney Bean
- *Best cooking:* Skadi
- *Best for families:* Angel's
- *Best happy-hour menu:* Mammoth Brewing Company (a.k.a. Whiskey Creek)
- *Best Mexican:* Roberto's
- *Best newcomer:* Petra's
- *Best romantic night out:* The Restaurant at Convict Lake
- *Best seafood:* Ocean Harvest
- *Best value:* Base Camp Cafe
- *Best wine bistro:* Petra's

Eating in

For thousands of visitors to Mammoth and June, most nights are spent eating in. The typical visiting family or group stays in a kitchen-equipped condo or cabin, and it's just more cost-effective to stay in most nights.

That said, not everyone feels like cooking a big feast after a hard day on the slopes or the trails. Because one of the Eastern Sierra's few shortcomings is the lack of a Trader Joe's, we often bring a cooler stocked with its quality, bargain-priced food, from wine to Clif Bars to frozen entrees ready to heat for an easy dinner—and we're not above bringing up one of those Stouffer's frozen lasagnas from the Smart & Final in Bishop.

The only Mammoth pizza place that delivers is Domino's, which I consider acceptable only if the adults are going out and it's just for the kids, whose tastebuds are not yet fully formed. A better option, if you don't want to go out to pick up pizza, is to call Doorstep Dinners (760-934-3463), which represents two better places than Domino's.

By the time you read this, the lovely little Village Market, source of good cheeses and quality foods, will have been torn down to make way for a hulking fractional-ownership development. So Vons will be the only market in town. It's a good Vons, typically well stocked, but be warned that on Friday evenings and throughout holiday weekends in ski season, it can suddenly resemble a food co-op in East Berlin before the collapse of the wall. One Presidents Day weekend, I waltzed into Vons about 10 p.m. on Friday night to find the huge bread aisle completely empty. Not a slice of white or wheat. Not even a slice of the weird breads. Nothing. During these busy times, the aisles are so clogged with dazed skiers and boarders that you might be willing to do without food for the weekend. If you're headed up on a Friday night and haven't brought condo or cabin supplies from home, consider stocking up in Bishop instead. It has a Vons, a Smart & Final and the locally owned Joseph's Bi-Rite market.

Bars & pub grub

The Clocktower
6080 Minaret Rd., Mammoth
(760) 934-2725
Open nightly 4 p.m.–1:30 a.m.

A collegiate-style pub underneath the Alpenhof's clock tower, this is the sort of place where boisterous young outdoorspeople drink lots of beer and play foosball. It's a local's favorite, free of the attitude at more upscale "clubs" like Fever and a fun place to meet friends for a lively gathering after a day on the mountain. Amusements include a pool table, foosball, pinball, darts and big-screen TV.

Lakanuki
The Village, 6201 Minaret Rd., Mammoth
(760) 934-7447
Bar open daily 11 a.m.–1:30 p.m.

If you're 23 and looking for nooky (get it? like-a-nooky?), this happening ersatz tiki bar in the new Village might be just the ticket. If you're over 30, you might be sorry. If you're over 40, you'll seem pathetic.

Roberto's
271 Old Mammoth Rd., Mammoth
(760) 934-3667
Open daily 11 a.m.–10 p.m.

The new upstairs cantina at Roberto's became a hot spot the minute it opened. Although many of the people sitting at the bar or one of the high tables are waiting to eat downstairs, plenty are there just for a drink, and for good reason—the bartenders make the best margarita in town. Roberto's is convivial and comfortable, with a TV for sports and big windows bringing in mountain and sunset views. The bar menu is excellent, offering things like lobster burritos and duck tacos.

Mammoth Brewing Company

Upstairs at Whiskey Creek
Main St. & Minaret Rd., Mammoth
(760) 934-2337
Open nightly 4 p.m.–varies (perhaps 9 p.m. on quiet weeknights, 2 a.m. on
busy weekends

Hands down the best happy-hour eating in town is above Whiskey Creek, in the bar/brewpub that shares the same owner and kitchen as the fancier downstairs restaurant. All my friends' great fear is that if Whiskey Creek sells (both this location and the one in Bishop are on the market as I write this), new owners will change the happy hour. From 4 to 5:30 p.m. every day, the excellent bar menu is half price, as are the bar's own brews on tap—and they're good brews. So you can have, for instance, a pint of the excellent Amber Ale, the delicious wasabi-crusted ahi salad and some salmon spring rolls, a terrific meal for less than $14. The salads are tasty, the steak sandwich with grilled onions and red peppers is messy and wonderful, the grilled portobello sandwich makes vegetarians happy, and if they have clam chowder, it's a good one. You can even get a flatiron steak with mashed potatoes and asparagus for less than $10—if you get your order in before 5:30. But hey, who isn't ready to think of dinner at 5 when you've been active outdoors all day! As for the bar, it's a comfortable place with different seating areas, barstools, a pool table and a little bandstand area; weekends often bring live music. If you come early (i.e. for happy hour), the place is kid-friendly—my kids love the burgers and Caesar salads.

Petra's Wine Bar & Coffeehouse

6080 Minaret Rd., Mammoth
(760) 934-3500
Open Tues.–Sun. 5:30–10 p.m. (kitchen closes at 9 p.m.)

See listing under "Upscale Dining,"page 89.

The Yodler

Across from Main Lodge, Mammoth Mountain
(760) 934-0636
Open daily in spring, summer & fall 11 a.m.–5 p.m.; in winter 11 a.m.–9 p.m.
*   closing time varies depending on business*

Happy are the people sitting on the Yodler's large terrace on a sunny afternoon, sipping a Sam Adams, listening to music, sharing the Mammoth nachos and comparing notes on their ski runs, bike rides or hikes of the day. Located between Main Lodge and the Mammoth Mountain Inn, just behind the climbing tower (which winter sometimes buries in snow), this Mammoth institution is, along with the Clocktower, one of the places to meet friends at the end of a mountain day. The beer selection is good, the wine selection not so good, and the Irish coffee just the ticket on cold days. Families take note: This is one kid-friendly pub, with a good $5.95 kids' menu. The pub grub—fish tacos, burgers, ribs, chicken wings, chili—is pretty heavy stuff, but it goes well with the beer. Prices are reasonable, given the location.

Breakfast, **coffee**
& grazing

Base Camp Café

3325 Main St., Mammoth
(760) 934-3900
Open Mon.–Wed. 7:30 a.m.–3 p.m., Thurs.–Sat. 7:30 a.m.–8 p.m.,
*   Sun. 7:30 a.m.–9 p.m.*

See review under "Best Mid-Range Restaurants."

Blondie's

3599 Main St., Mammoth
(760) 934-4048
Open daily 6:30 a.m.–1 p.m.

Blondie is actually a redhead, and her place has a redhead's zest and personality. Done in bright white and red, with Mary Engelbreit wallpaper, goofy pots of fake sunflowers, and white wooden booths, this is my favorite place in town to wake up. The coffee is robust, the service is friendly, and the food is terrific: cinnamony French toast with a berry compote, homemade waffles, dreamy homemade biscuits and gravy, excellent fresh orange juice and four-egg omelets and scrambles that are a protein-loader's dream. Lunchtime brings good sandwiches, soups, salads and burgers.

The Breakfast Club
Old Mammoth Rd. & Main St., Mammoth
(760) 934-6944
Open daily 6 a.m.–1 p.m.
No credit cards

A close rival with Blondie's for best breakfast in town, this place is known for its baked goods, especially the muffins and sweet rolls. Also terrific are its eggs with smoked linguica sausage, its pancakes, its Baja scramble and its three-egg omelets. This bustling café is jam-packed on weekends, so get there early or late or be prepared for a wait. It's quieter at lunch, when regulars order the Cabo tacos, burritos and sandwiches.

The Looney Bean
Rite Aid Center, Old Mammoth Rd., Mammoth
(760) 934-1345
Open Sun.–Thurs. 5:45 a.m.–7 p.m., Fri.–Sat. 5:45 a.m.–9 p.m.

The local's coffeehouse of choice, the Looney Bean recently had to leave its comfortably ramshackle old cottage for the relative sterility of a strip mall. But while the new space is shinier and spiffier, it still has the same great Looney Bean vibe—this ain't no generic Starbucks. And now there's a wonderful stone fireplace for cold days. The coffee is superb, there's good music on the stereo, and the baked goods are delicious (try the cinnamon drop scone). Outside are several tables, where dogs doze in the sun and kids scamper about. Bring a book, or pick up one from the little in-house library and hang awhile with your double-shot latte.

Old New York Deli & Bagel Co.
The Village, 6201 Minaret Rd., Ste. 105, Mammoth
(760) 924-2457
Open daily 6:30 a.m.–9 p.m.

The Village is a long way from Brooklyn, but the bagels here are nonetheless made in the authentic way, with a dense chewiness. The espresso drinks are good, too. The menu goes far beyond bagels, offering lots of breakfast classics (French toast, eggs with lox), tasty deli sandwiches, burgers, salads and delicious small pizzas. I wanted to dislike this place because it seems to represent the shiny "new" Mammoth, but it really does a good job and has been embraced by many locals. Laptop owners take note that the WiFi is free here. Now if they would just turn off that annoying pseudo-jazz and put on some decent music....

Starbucks

The Village, 6201 Minaret Rd., Mammoth
(760) 934-2202

Old Mammoth Rd. & Meridian, Mammoth
(760) 924-5057

Inside Von's, Minaret Village Mall, Old Mammoth Rd., Mammoth
(760) 934-4536

Now that Starbucks is invading even China, there probably isn't a person alive who doesn't know a vente no-foam latte from a tall half-caff mocha. If you want personality and local character, go to the Looney Bean or the Breakfast Club. If you want the double-tall nonfat latte that you're hooked on, go to one of these Mammoth Starbucks.

Eating on the **mountain**

Canyon Beach Bar & BBQ

On the patio at Canyon Lodge, Mammoth Mountain
No phone
Open for lunch daily during ski season

There are two patios in front of Canyon Lodge, one with this bar and outdoor grill and the other without. Not surprisingly, scoring a sunny-day table on the bar-and-grill side is an epic achievement. The thing to eat here is the tri-tip sandwich—not as good as the real thing down in San Luis Obispo, to be sure, but a mighty welcome sight after a morning on the mountain. The partially precooked burgers are less appealing. Some people get so comfortable with a beer and a sandwich that they have another beer, then another, then decide that they didn't really feel like boarding the rest of the afternoon anyway.

Marketplace Food Court

McCoy Station, Mammoth Mountain
Open for breakfast & lunch daily

When the old Mid-Chalet was gussied up and renamed McCoy Station a few years ago, the food got better, too. Yes, it's a cafeteria, and of course it's too expensive, but much of the food is quite satisfying. I'm partial to the stir-fries, either the kung pao chicken or the Mongolian beef with veggies. The burritos are hearty (split one with a pal), the fruit is surprisingly good (they get sweet, juicy oranges), and the coffee's from Starbucks.

Outpost BBQ

Bottom of Chair 14, Mammoth Mountain
Open for lunch daily mid-Dec.–early April

Are the chili dogs really better at the Outpost? Are the chips any crisper, the sodas any colder? Of course not—and yet, everything just tastes better over here on Mammoth's hidden backside, behind Scotty's and the top of poky old Chair 12. Or rather, it all tastes fabulous on a bluebird day, when you're sitting out on the patio, soaking in the sun, the incredible beauty of the setting and the buzz of the runs you just made down Arriba and Santiago. On a snowy, wind-whipped day, lunch at the Outpost, which has only outdoor terrace seating, can be a grueling affair.

On good-weather weekends, get there by 11:30 to stake out a table and get in line at the order window. The menu is limited to burgers, hot dogs, chili dogs, chili bowls and accompaniments. If you brown-bag it, no one minds—a PB&J tastes better over here, too.

Parallax

McCoy Station, Mammoth Mountain
(760) 934-2571, ext. 3118
Open for lunch daily during ski season 11 a.m.–3 p.m.

When the former Mid-Chalet morphed into the snazzier McCoy Station, a snazzy new restaurant appeared, too. Parallax is a serious dining room smack in the middle of the mountain, with awesome views of the top-of-the-mountain runs, the Minarets and peaks galore. The mountain brought in chef Bryan Doi from Hawaii, and he turns out a Cal-Asian cuisine modified for the snow instead of the surf. Try the poke-style ceviche martini, with citrus-marinated seafood, avocado and roasted pepper; the pepper-seared ahi Caesar salad; or the tasty flat-iron steak sandwich with watercress, tomatoes, caramelized onions and roquefort.

At press time, word was that chef Doi might not be returning, so be warned that the menu and quality could change for the 2005 season. If that's true, he'll be missed, as will his two dogs—they romp every day on McCoy's roof, amusing skiers and boarders below, sometimes even deliberately pushing snow down on people who taunt them.

Mid-range restaurants

Angel's
3516 Main St., Mammoth
(760) 934-7427
Open daily 11:30 a.m.–9 p.m.; closing time varies depending on business

Locals worried when this long-popular, family-friendly place changed hands recently, but their fears were unfounded. The new owners clearly know what they're doing, and the result is a constant crowd waiting for a table in the folksy, knotty-pine dining room and bar. Warm, well-trained servers deliver huge portions of tasty American food that really hits the spot after a day outdoors: fantastic biscuits, served instead of the usual boring bread; tender, succulent ribs and chicken smoked over orangewood; restorative homemade soups; thin, crispy onion rings (really more onion strings); hearty tostada, Cobb and Asian salads; and good burgers, wraps and sandwiches (triple-stacked grilled club, ortega chile melt, tuna-avocado melt, etc.). Worth the wait.

Base Camp Café
3325 Main St., Mammoth
(760) 934-3900
Open Mon.–Wed. 7:30 a.m.–3 p.m., Thurs.–Sat. 7:30 a.m.–8 p.m.,
     Sun. 7:30 a.m.–9 p.m.

This friendly locals' hangout is the best deal in town for hungry outdoors folks. The cooking is hearty, tasty and bargain-priced by Mammoth standards: a cup of three-bean chili or homemade soup for $3.50, meal-size sandwiches for $6.95, a bagel with egg, bacon and cheese for $3.95, a turkey-avocado salad for $7.95, a sirloin steak for $12.95. They'll also fix you a sack lunch with a first-rate sandwich, to take hiking or skiing, for $7.95. They make a good cup of coffee and a proper latte, too.

Berger's
6118 Minaret Rd., Mammoth
(760) 934-6622
Open daily 11:30 a.m.–9 p.m. (sometimes 9:30 p.m.)

You eat burgers at Berger's, or maybe a French dip or tri-tip sandwich. A long-established local's favorite across Minaret from the new Village, this is a bright, cheerful place with a woodsy interior and brisk service. The meats are good, the burgers are indeed tasty, the salads are just fine, and the prices are reasonable. A reliable standby.

Giovanni's

Minaret Village Mall, Old Mammoth Rd. & Meridian, Mammoth
(760) 934-7563
Deliveries: (760) 934-3463 (Doorstep Dinners)
Open Mon.–Sat. 11 a.m.–9 p.m., Sun. 4–9 p.m.; may stay open later if
business warrants

Instead of joining in the perennial argument about which Mammoth pizza is better, Giovanni's or Nik 'n' Willy's, let me just recommend them both. Giovanni's is better if you want to eat there—it has a fair number of red-check-clothed tables and good service. It's also a little less expensive. (Pizza is shockingly expensive in Mammoth.) And it has some worthwhile creative pizzas, like the small one topped with Alpers smoked trout, capers, red onion, cucumber and dill cream cheese, or the spicy Thai, with chicken or tofu, peanut sauce, cilantro, corn and red onion. You can also get a classic thin-crust cheese pizza, a decent salad and a good lasagna or plate of spaghettini al pesto. All pizzas can be ordered "take and bake"—which comes with a fifteen-percent discount—so you can eat them hot from your own oven.

Gomez's

Mountain Blvd. (off Main St. behind the Texaco), Mammoth
(760) 924-2693
Open daily 11:30 a.m.–9:30 p.m.

A local's hangout, Gomez's is full of funky, old-Mammoth charm. It occupies a worn A-frame cabin, with a buzzing dining room in front and a small bar in back, where mountain-man regulars tell stories and play the get-the-ring-on-the-nail-in-the-wall game (it's addictive). The cooking is standard melted-cheese Mexican, sometimes a little bland but sometimes quite tasty; the garlicky camarones al mojo de ajo are perhaps the best thing on the menu, and the huevos dishes are also good. Tequila connoisseurs, take note that the bar pours 30 different ones. Service is rapid, and prices are modest, especially for the combination plates.

Matsu

3711 Main St., Mammoth
(760) 934-8277
Open Mon.–Fri. 11:30 a.m.–9 p.m., Sat.–Sun. 4:30–9 p.m.

This little house has an appealing, modestly priced menu of pan-Asian dishes, from veggie stir-fries to Chinese chicken salad to Thai-style mint chili. Unfortunately, new owners have allowed the quality to slip. The menu says the teriyaki ribs are "famous," but they're actually kind of tough and uninspired, served with enough white rice to give Dr. Atkins a heart attack. Better bets are the tasty tofu rice bowl; the stir-fried vegetable bowl; the pansit, a Filipino dish of noodles stir-fried with shrimp, pork, snow peas, onion and a bit of lemon and vinegar for tang; and the soups. There seems to be a Hawaiian influence, as evidenced by the aforementioned ribs with a mountain of white rice and the saimin noodle soup, a Hawaiian staple. No more full bar, but the sake is hot and the beer is cold. Let's hope the new owners bring Matsu back to its former standards soon.

The Mogul Steakhouse

1528 Tavern Rd. (off Old Mammoth Rd.), Mammoth
(760) 934-3039
Open nightly 5:30–9 p.m.; hours extended for holidays & busy weekends

An always-reliable place for a steak dinner, the Mogul is a Mammoth fixture of some 30 years' standing. It's a woodsy, mountain-lodgy sort of place, with a relaxed drinking bar and a large salad bar (which is included with most entrees). Although the kitchen turns out fresh fish, pork, chicken, pasta and broiled shrimp, the thing to get here is red meat: grilled center-cut top sirloin, New York steak, a delicious porterhouse (big enough to share), prime rib and rack of lamb. The grill chefs generally cook the meat just right. The desserts are the sort of things you're best advised to share: almond-mocha fudge ice cream pie, cheesecake, hot fudge sundaes. The Mogul isn't cheap, but it's fairly priced by local standards and the wine list is a bargain. Also, if you arrive between 5:30 and 6, your entrée will cost $2 less. Parents take note that the kids' menu includes the salad bar, instead of the usual unhealthy, all-fried kids' meals.

Nik 'n' Willy's Pizza & Subs

76 Old Mammoth Rd., Mammoth
(760) 934-2012
Deliveries: (760) 934-3463 (Doorstep Dinners)
Open daily 11:30 a.m.–9 p.m.

This locals' favorite is growing more popular by the day—new branches popped up recently in Bishop and Lone Pine. I get put off by the prices—$27.75 for a sixteen-inch Thai chicken pizza is mighty steep—but the pies taste great. So do the hot sub sandwiches, from the BLT to the Yardbird, with chicken, bacon, onions, pickles, provolone and more. At $6 to $8, the lunch specials are a better value. And if you're counting pennies, look for the coupons offering a free salad—they seem to be plentiful around town.

Savvy regulars, hungry after a day outdoors, call Nik 'n' Willy's from the mountain and order a "take-and-bake" pizza, which costs fifteen percent less. Then they fire up the oven back at the condo and have fresh, hot pizza after everyone's done with the hot tub and the showers. You can also eat at the restaurant, but it's not much of a setting.

Ocean Harvest

248 Old Mammoth Rd.
(760) 934-8539
Open nightly 5:30–9 p.m.

Long considered the best seafood restaurant in Mammoth, Ocean Harvest is for sale as I write this, so its future is uncertain. As of today, it remains an excellent value for a fresh-fish dinner: Prices range from $13.95 for Pacific red snapper to $19.95 for Norwegian salmon, and dinners come with sourdough bread, salad or clam chowder, vegetables and rice or potatoes; early birds who arrive before 6 p.m. get a discount. This is not sophisticated stuff—the fish is simply grilled over mesquite, done Cajun or Jamaican style if you like, or perhaps with a flavored butter (try the pesto butter). If you don't feel like fish, take note that Ocean Harvest just won the rib cook-off in town, so try its pork baby-back ribs. Worthwhile appetizers include the bucket of steamed clams with garlic butter and the smoked salmon. The setting is wood upon wood: wooden tables, wooden captain's chairs and wood-paneled walls; windows bring in mountain views.

Perry's Italian Cafe

3399 Main St., Mammoth
(760) 934-6521
Open for breakfast daily 7 a.m.–11 a.m., for lunch & dinner daily 11 a.m.–9 p.m.;
closing hours later if business warrants

I'm no great fan of Perry's, but my kids insisted that I include it in this book. They love the vintage video games by the bar (bring quarters), the kid-friendly vibe (tons of families come here), the garlic bread (it's decadent) and the kids' menu (it's basic, just the way kids like it). The folks here are congenial, working hard to accommodate the steady stream of hungry people; the prices are low by Mammoth standards; and the Italian food is fine in a generic sort of way: spaghetti with meatballs, chicken piccata, eggplant parmigiana, hearty hot sub sandwiches and traditional pizzas. Avoid the fancier or more complicated dishes and you'll be fine. A good value.

Roberto's Cafe

271 Old Mammoth Rd., Mammoth
(760) 934-3667
Open daily 11 a.m.–10 p.m.

There's always a wait for a table at this Mammoth hot spot, so finally the owners added a second floor, creating a bright, open cantina so people can get comfortable and have a margarita (or a Shirley Temple—this is a popular family place) while they wait. Many regulars end up giving up the wait for a table downstairs and order from the bar menu, which is actually more appealing than the main menu (try the duck quesadilla and lobster tacos). Otherwise this is classic California-Mexican, gooey and cheesy and hard to resist. The homemade tortillas, quality meats and good margaritas make this the best Mexican restaurant in town.

Shogun

Sierra Center Mall, 2nd floor
Old Mammoth Rd., Mammoth
(760) 934-3970
Open nightly 5 p.m.–9:30 p.m.; closing may vary depending on season & business

If you live in the Eastern Sierra and don't get much opportunity to have good sushi and Japanese food, Shogun is fine. But it pales in comparison to the Japanese food enjoyed by Angelenos and San Franciscans. Not worth going out of your way for, but if you're jonesing for a California roll or a salmon teriyaki dinner, it'll suffice. The dining room is pleasant, with a fine view of the mountains, and the bar can be fun, especially on karaoke nights (Tuesdays, Saturdays and holiday weekends).

Upscale dining

Eagle's Landing

Double Eagle Resort & Spa
5587 Hwy. 158 (June Lake Loop), June Lake Loop
(760) 648-7897
www.doubleeagleresort.com
Open daily 11:30 a.m.–4:30 p.m. & 5:30–9:30 p.m., breakfast Fri.–Sun.
    7 a.m.–11:30 a.m.

Mountain restaurants don't get much more attractive than this, so it's a shame that the food and service don't live up to the promise. Touted as the luxury restaurant on the June Lake Loop, Eagle's Landing is part of the beautiful Double Eagle Resort & Spa, nestled under imposing Carson Peak, with Reversed Creek running through the property. The large, pine-paneled dining room has soaring ceilings, huge windows bringing in mountain and waterfall views, a cozy bar and a lovely outdoor terrace for summertime lunch. Lunch is a better bet here—the simpler salads and sandwiches are just fine, and they taste even better in such a great setting. But I've found anything more complicated than the basic Caesar salad to be disappointing. The chef is fond of overly sweet flavors, as with the coconut shrimp and the macadamia-crusted halibut that is proudly pitched as being done in a bananas foster style. The orange-glazed salmon was both too sweet and too sour at the same time; the wild rice pilaf served with many dishes just didn't taste right; and the crème brulee was leaden, the top barely tanned, let alone crunchy. I hope the management can bring Eagle's Landing up to the promise of the setting, the prices and the hype.

Lakefront Restaurant

Tamarack Lodge, Lake Mary Rd., Mammoth
(760) 934-3534
Open daily in summer 11 a.m.–2 p.m. & 5:30–9:30 p.m.
In fall, winter & spring, open Sat.–Sun. 11 a.m.–2 p.m., nightly 5:30–9:30 p.m.

I used to think that this pricey, upscale restaurant, part of the main lodge in the Tamarack collection of cabins, was too old-school, fussy French. But a couple of recent meals have changed my mind. One was a summer lunch on the sunny terrace overlooking Twin Lakes; the trout may have been from Idaho instead of Tim Alpers' ranch, but it was fantastic, with a crisp skin and a lovely butter sauce. The fluffy quiche was pretty fab, too. Another was a dinner inside the small, knotty-pine-paneled dining room, where I had a mighty good rack of lamb and lavender-scented vanilla crème brulee. The Lakefront is too expensive for ordinary dinners, but if you're having a romantic retreat at one of Tamarack's cabins, you could do far worse than to walk to this dining room and indulge a little.

Nevados

Main St. & Minaret Rd., Mammoth
(760) 934-4466
Open nightly 5:30–9 p.m.; closing time varies depending on the season & business

A warm, friendly place run by Tim Dawson, Nevados attracts a crowd that knows their tartare from their gravlax and has the financial wherewithal to order both. The small bar is a good spot to meet for a drink if you're too over-30 for Clocktower or Dublin's, and the two intimate dining spaces, notable for their skillful lighting and lively trompe l'oeil mural along one wall, are always full, so make reservations as soon as you can. The kitchen knows what it's doing: The roasted elk loin is tender and savory, the osso buco is meaty and succulent, the panko-fried soft-shell crab is irresistible, and the warm pear and almond tart with caramel sauce and vanilla ice cream is heaven. Service is professional. This is a pricey place, so at $40, the three-course prix-fixe dinner is almost a bargain.

Petra's Wine Bar

6080 Minaret Rd., Mammoth
(760) 934-3500
Open Tues.–Sun. 5:30–9 p.m. for dinner; dessert & wine served until 10 p.m.

Robert and Kirk Schaubmayer, sons of the longtime owners of the Alpenhof motel, were ready to take on their own project, so they shut down the venerable old Matterhorn restaurant next to the motel and created Mammoth's first real wine bar. Named for their mother, who died of cancer a couple of years ago, Petra's is an outstanding addition to the Mammoth food and drink scene. The setting is inviting, with a mix of high bar-style tables, roomy regular tables and a long hand-hewn wooden bar counter; lighting is flattering; and swell vintage ski posters line the walls. Wine by the glass takes center stage here; you can have one-and-a-half- or three-ounce tastings or conventional six-ounce glasses (or, of course, an entire bottle if you'd rather). These aren't the usual sauvignon blancs and merlots—a recent offering included a superb Morgan pinot noir, a lovely sparkling Spanish cava (a bargain at $5.50 a glass), an intriguing if pricey Villa Russiz pinot grigio, and the Justin Obtuse port from Paso Robles.

Ah, but wine without food is like a meadow without wildflowers, so it's a good thing the kitchen knows what it's doing. Every night there's a short list of dishes designed to be shared as well as to pair with wine: perhaps a few Fanny Bay oysters, a seductive Tuscan white bean soup with a drizzle of basil pesto, a hearty bruschetta, a tender piece of Alaskan halibut encrusted with olives, served with a roasted tomato coulis and baby spinach, and a yummy lemon napoleon.

Although the prices aren't terribly high, and you can graze and sip for a modest investment, it's also easy to get carried away, ordering a couple more little wine tastes here and another savory little dish there...until the tab mounts quickly. That's why Petra's is listed under "Upscale Dining," even though it's a pretty casual (if stylish) place.

The Restaurant at Convict Lake

Convict Lake Resort
Rte. 1, off Hwy. 395, just south of Mammoth Airport
(760) 934-3803
Open nightly 5:30–9 p.m.; closing time varies depending on business;
*   lunch in summer daily 11:30 a.m.–2:30 p.m.*

This place is *almost* the perfect luxury mountain restaurant—it's missing just a few things. There's no espresso machine, for instance, which is baffling; annoying pseudo-jazz plays in the bar; and the dining room is too dark. But these are mere quibbles, for if truth be told, I can't wait to return for another memorable dinner—or a summertime lunch on the lawn, under the aspen trees.

The setting is delicious: wine-colored leather banquettes, paneled walls, thick white linens and a gleaming copper-sheathed fireplace in the center of the main dining room; a couple of smaller dining rooms offer privacy for groups or romancers. The bar has deep leather club chairs, a game table and a TV, making it a swell place to hang out before or after dinner.

Chef Matt Eoff calls his cuisine "country French," and it is indeed French in inspiration and execution, although American, Asian and Mediterranean influences are also present. His multiculturalism is evident in such appetizers as the tasting of "island fishes," which includes Scottish gravlax, Hawaiian ahi tartare and seared Fijian albacore. Less successful was the ravioli of duck confit, a large ravioli that really shouldn't have been deep-fried.

Eoff changes his menu often, so there's no telling what you'll be offered, but he's known for certain entrees that are generally available: seared rainbow trout from local Alpers Ranch, perhaps flavored with garlic, scallions, sun-dried tomatoes, almonds and a chardonnay butter sauce; a classic beef wellington, wonderfully decadent; lamb osso buco, braised with leeks and served over pasta; giant prawns, perhaps done Asian style with baby bok choy, coconut green-curry broth and red ginger; and fresh salmon, perhaps paired with a beurre blanc spiked with osetra caviar. Desserts are lovely: chocolate ganache, crème caramel, various banana creations, fruit strudels and so forth.

The wine list has won awards, including from Wine Spectator magazine, and not only is the collection smart, it's also quite fairly priced.

Skadi
Sherwin Plaza 3, 2nd floor
Old Mammoth Rd. & Chateau Rd., Mammoth
(760) 934-3902
Open Wed.–Sun. 5:30 p.m.–9:30 p.m.

I have always been wary of Scandinavian cuisine, being able to tolerate only tiny amounts of dill, the national herb of Scandinavia. But Norwegian owner/ chef Ian Algeroen has perfected his own brand of modern Sierra cooking, with a subtle Scandinavian influence and a reliance on local products—many of which come from Walking Beam Ranch in Santa Paula. The menu changes often with the seasons and the availability of ingredients; good examples of his cooking include a gorgeously arranged seafood sampler; carefully composed salads; a classic French choucroute (sauerkraut) made with jagerwurst and venison sausage from Walking Beam; a simple, crisp-skinned salmon with brown butter and pine nuts; and a superb lamb shank, tender but not fatty, steeped in garlic, rosemary and red wine. The duck breast on a bed of lingonberries is pretty fab, too. To drink with all this, you'll find some interesting smaller-label wines, many of which are too rich for my wallet, but a few of which are affordable. At evening's end, live a little and splurge on dessert—the crème brulee and the tasting of chocolate desserts are worth every calorie.

You'll eat all this good stuff in an intimate room that is much lovelier than the ugly-strip-mall setting would suggest: a dramatic open-raftered ceiling, good lighting, well-set tables and, most of all, huge windows bringing in superb mountain views. Although I've heard a few complaints about service, I've always been very well cared for. And I always look forward to the next time a special occasion warrants dropping the big bucks for the best cooking in town.

Whiskey Creek
Main St. & Minaret Rd., Mammoth
(760) 934-2555
Open nightly 5 p.m.–8:30 p.m., later during busy times

This old favorite in Mammoth has done a swell job of staying fresh. A remodel several years ago showcases the gleaming tanks of the in-house brewery (which makes several very good beers) and created comfortable seating areas on two floors (not counting the upstairs bar, Mammoth Brewing Company, which has its own review under "Bars & Pub Grub"). The wine list is decent and fairly priced, the bartenders make a good cocktail, and the kitchen has been in fine form lately. Try the seductive fondue of brie, roquefort and caramelized onions served with prosciutto-wrapped apples, grilled asparagus and toasted bread; the spinach salad with walnut-crusted goat cheese; the cola-marinated pork chops; the vegetarian platter, with miso-soy vegetables and a cranberry-rice pilaf; any of the steaks; and the seared rare ahi with teriyaki beurre blanc. If only it weren't quite so expensive...but, hey, that's life in Mammoth.

TWELVE SECRETS TO
SKIING & BOARDING MAMMOTH
(& JUNE)

They said it was too far from a metropolitan area, it was too high in altitude, it was too remote from any road or town, there were no facilities. They said it wasn't what people were accustomed to—too much snow, too windy, too rugged. They said Mammoth could not be tamed.

— Dave McCoy, quoted in *Mammoth, The Sierra Legend*

You'd have to try hard to have a bad time on the slopes of Mammoth Mountain. (Or June Mountain.) But you'll have a truly memorable time if you do it like the locals do. Read on to learn how to make the most of your Mammoth skiing and boarding time.

Best secret
runs

Some Mammoth runs seem crowded even on Tuesdays, especially those that funnel people from several other runs. Regulars all know, for instance, the bitter irony of the name of the run Solitude—its lower part is a merging spot for people coming off of Goldrush and Chair 5, as well as those coming off the backside of chairs 25 and 22, and it's typically a swarming anthill.

Here are my favorite quieter Mammoth runs during busy periods:

Least challenging
Near Roller Coaster (a.k.a. Chair 4) lies a hidden area serviced by Chair 20, which isn't often in service. But during the busiest times, such as Presidents Day weekend, **Chair 20** is fired up, and there's never a wait. The once-green run called **Merry Go Round** is now a jib run for boarders, with rolling jumps and a couple of rails, but it's usu-ally empty, and you can avoid the jumps and cruise the easy terrain around them. Or live a little and go up and down the smaller bumps—if you keep your speed in check, you won't get any air, but you'll have a fun roller-coaster ride.

Off the Little Eagle chair, stay on the far left and find the run called **Bridges**—it's an easy blue that's often empty. Tree lovers will have a blast darting in and out of the woods along Bridges. It's been a favorite of my kids for years.

More challenging
For some reason, **Wall Street,** one of Mammoth's great blue-black groomed cruisers, rarely gets crowded, except for occasional clumps of people. (Just wait a minute and they'll pass.) It's found behind the big Mammoth sign near the top of the Canyon Express and Roller Coaster chairs.

On the backside, chairs 13 and 14 access some wonderful blue-black runs, especially **Arriba, Surprise** and **Santiago,** and they are generally pretty uncrowded.

It's slow as molasses, but the old two-person Chair 21, on the other side of the Mill Café from the Goldrush chair, is usually empty, even on Presidents Day weekend. Its primary run, **Lost in the Woods,** is a good place to ditch the crowds. Although labeled blue, it's more of a green, except for one short, steeper part.

My personal favorite—and I am loathe to share this—is **Coyote,** an arcing, perfectly pitched steep groomer that is hard to find, even though it's quite visible to those riding Chair 5 and Goldrush. It's reached via Chair 3 (Facelift Express), but it's invisible from any of 3's runs until you're right on top of it. Stay to the skier's far right of the face of 3 and ski China Bowl, which can have challenging bumps and/ or thick snow—but in fresh, light snow, it's a dream. Keep heading straight down, past the stinky sulfur vent (a little reminder that Mammoth remains an active volcano), toward what looks like a dead end into trees. Coyote opens up on the right. Yee-ha!

Most challenging

The crowds thin out pretty much everywhere on the top except Cornice, the run that every improving intermediate has to "prove" him- or herself on. If you're a true expert, head over to **Paranoid Flats,** which rarely has more than three people on it. Because of its relative isolation, **Dave's** (named for Mammoth founder Dave McCoy) is almost always a good bet for great snow, a steep pitch, a top-of-the-world feeling and minimal crowds; an advanced but not expert skier can enjoy Dave's. If there's fresh snow and you're an accomplished powder hound, head for the tree steeps on the backside (**Chair 14**) or the **Dragon's Back** or **Wazoo** runs off Chair 9.

June Mountain

Crowds? What crowds? Every run at June is typically uncrowded. There's no "secret" run here. The entire mountain is a secret.

Early bird gets
the **fun**

No one likes sleeping in more than I do. But I save my sleeping in for other sorts of vacations—when I'm skiing in Mammoth on weekends or holidays, I get up early. Hell, even my sleep-obsessed teenage daughter gets up early, too. And if you want to have a good ski day, you'll get your butt out of bed, too. The reasons are varied:

→ The runs are relatively empty from 8:30 to 10 a.m., and you're likely to get your best skiing of the day in during that time, especially if you follow the sun (see next page). At 10, hordes of parents drop off kids at ski school, and the hungover and slow movers appear, and suddenly there are people everywhere.

→ If you're driving, you can find parking on weekends and holidays only if you head out very early. Otherwise forget it.

→ An early breakfast followed by a few hours of skiing means you'll be ready for lunch at 11:30—so eat your lunch while the lodges are empty and everyone else is still doing warm-up runs. Then when they all come in for lunch later (ski school gets out at 1, so that's rush hour), you can ski less-crowded runs from 12:30 to 2.

→ You can quit early and avoid those 4 p.m. rush-hour crowds on the Canyon or Main Lodge runs. And you'll get a spot in the hot tub before everyone else.

There is one exception to the early-bird rule: When spring conditions arrive, usually in April, you can sleep in. There's no point in rushing out for first-morning ice. Wait until it softens and head out around 10. By spring the crowds have diminished anyway.

Follow the
sun

When the mountain is blessed with fresh powder, any place you can find fresh tracks is great. But on a more typical packed-powder or spring-skiing day, the smart people follow the sun. In the morning, start on Lincoln Mountain, where the sun first hits the snow. On crusty mornings, the snow softens first here. If you're an expert, head for Chair 9; Chair 25 has great advanced-intermediate runs (Back for More is my favorite) and a wonderful intermediate cruiser (Quicksilver); and Little Eagle is rich with beginner and easy-intermediate terrain.

On sunny days, the snow on the east side of Lincoln will start slushing up after a couple of hours, so that's the time to start working your way around the mountain. Strong skiers and boarders can take a high route: Chair 5 for awhile, then Chair 3, then 23 or the gondola to the top, then, if you have time, over to the backside, Chairs 13 and 14. Less confident skiers can take a lower route: Chair 17 or 8, then Canyon Express or Roller Coaster, then Broadway Express or Chair 7 and perhaps over to Chair 12 if you have time. The snow will soften as you move your way around the mountain, and you'll be gone from the sun-baked areas by the time it turns slushy.

Get me to the slopes
on time

If you are fortunate enough to own a slopeside condo or cabin, or the means to rent one, then you get to skip this section—you can ski or board right from your door. But if you're like the rest of us and can only afford a place off the mountain, you'll be taking part in that annual obsessive Mammoth conversation: Figuring out the best way to get on the mountain. Here are your three options, with their pros and cons.

On the shuttle

For most people on most days, Mammoth's free ski-season shuttle system (see map on page 224) is the best way to get to and from the lifts. The system is extensive, with stops near most of the condominium developments and motels.

The newish Village now serves as a shuttle hub, and at least based on the Village gondola's first season, it's a smart move to hop off there. Delivering you to the snow in front of Canyon Lodge, the gondola is fast and uncrowded (not to mention fun for kids).

My only problems with the shuttle have been on holiday weekends, notably King and Presidents Day. If you're shuttling those days, head out as early as possible, or after the 8 to 9:30 a.m. rush, or you may wait while many full buses roar by. To avoid long shuttle lines at the end of the day, quit an hour early or linger in the lodge with a beer or cocoa until the crowds thin.

Here are the main shuttle lines, with basic operating times for the ski season. Times may change somewhat; check www.mammothmountain.com for the latest information.

→ **Red Line:** Snowcreek Athletic Club to Main Lodge, via Old Mammoth Road, Main Street and Minaret; stops at Village hub. Runs 7 a.m.-5:30 p.m. At night, runs just between Snowcreek and the Village from 6 p.m.-11 p.m. (until midnight Friday, Saturday and holidays).

→ **Yellow Line:** Little Eagle to Canyon Lodge, via Majestic Pines, Kelley, Lake Mary Road and Lakeview; stops at Village hub. Runs 7:30 a.m.-5:30 p.m.; see Blue Line for night schedule.

→ **Blue Line:** The Canyon Lodge loop, from the Village to Canyon via Canyon Boulevard, heading back to the Village on Lakeview. Runs 7:15 a.m.-5:30 p.m. On Friday, Saturday and holiday nights, combines with Yellow Line to connect Canyon and Little Eagle via Canyon Boulevard, Minaret and Meridian, returning to Canyon Lodge via Lakeview; departs Canyon on the hour and Little Eagle on the half-hour.

→ **Green Line:** Old Mammoth commercial district to Little Eagle Lodge, via Meridian and Sierra Nevada Road; does not stop at the Village, but you can connect via the Red Line on Old Mammoth Road. Runs 7:30 a.m.-5:30 p.m.; does not run at night.

→ **Orange Line:** The Village to Tamarack Cross-Country Center. This line was discontinued for the 2003/2004 season but was recently reinstated. Runs 7:30 a.m.-5:30 p.m.; does not run at night. (This is how riders who ski out of bounds to Hole in the Wall get back to the lifts.)

In your car

As infuriating as it might be to discover that the snazzy new Village and its gondola were built with no public parking (parking is for Village residents and guests only), it was done for a reason. Both Intrawest and the town of Mammoth are trying to get us out of our cars. In part this is surely because they don't want to waste valuable lift-adjacent real estate on parking structures. To complicate matters, parking is forbidden on most town streets during ski season, for snow-removal reasons, so driving part way and parking near a shuttle stop is generally not feasible.

Besides, studies released as I write this showed that if we don't slow down global warming by using less fossil fuel, Sierra snowpack will drop 89% by the end of the century—so we can all do our part to ensure great future ski seasons by driving less.

That said, sometimes your car is the best way to go. If you're staying someplace off the shuttle line, or commuting from June, Tom's Place or Bishop, you'll need to drive. On the busiest holiday weekends, when the morning shuttles can get overwhelmed, my crew usually drives, stuffing as many people into a car as possible. (We park at a secret spot; I'd tell you, but then I'd have to kill you.)

All parking in the ski areas is free, except for the small up-front "premium" areas at Canyon and Main, which charge $15. And all the parking lots fill up early on weekends and holidays. The largest lot is found at Little Eagle, so your odds are best there. A popular parking area is the relatively small lot in front of Stump Alley—it has regulars that have met there for years, enjoying tailgate lunches and happy hours—but on weekends you need to get there by 7:30 (8 at the latest) to get a spot. The Canyon lot fills up fast—even the pay spots are gone by 8:15 on weekends, earlier on holidays. If you want to park at Canyon, get there at 7:30, snag a spot, then relax over coffee and a hot breakfast in the cafeteria. Main Lodge has perhaps the worst parking—cars line Minaret Road far down the hill, making for a long walk when you're carrying a lot of gear. And as of this writing, the Village has no all-day parking.

On foot

If your home base is near a lodge, consider walking. It's a great way to loosen up muscles before hitting the slopes, it helps acclimate you to the altitude, and it does the environment good.

The trick is to use the ski lockers. If you're staying near Canyon Lodge (which a great many people do), stop at the lodge when you first get into town. Park in the loading zone, head for the lower two floors and put your skis, poles, snowboards and helmets in the $1 lockers. (Keep your boots with you, so they don't get too chilly overnight.) Then each morning you can walk to Canyon without schlepping gear. (Snowboarders can wear their boots, and skiers can wear street shoes and carry their boots.) If the mountain is crowded, spend the extra $1 to keep your locker during the day, even if it's empty—then at quitting time you can stash your stuff and walk home, giving your tired muscles a much-needed cool-down stroll.

Unfortunately, ski lockers are not found at the Little Eagle lodge; at this writing they are not at the Village near the gondola, either, but they might be by 2005. Main Lodge has lockers, but because that area has no condos or houses, you won't be walking there.

Holiday hell...
and **heaven**

In a perfect world, none of us would go skiing on Presidents Day weekend or the day after Christmas. We'd have gobs of free time (with buckets of money, of course) to ski midweek to our heart's content. But the world isn't perfect—most of us have jobs, and many of us have kids in school. So we ski and board when we can—which means during the same holidays that 1,500 people are also waiting in line at Canyon Lodge.

I can't tell you every single one of my secrets for having a great holiday on the mountain—my friends have threatened grave penalties if I do—but I can tell you almost all of them. If you follow the Six Bs below, as my gang does, you'll get in tons of runs and have a wonderful time, despite the crowds:

THE SIX RULES OF
HOLIDAY SKI HEAVEN

1. **Buy lift tickets in advance.** If you aren't a pass holder, order your lift tickets on the phone (800-MAMMOTH). Then you can run into one of the lodges (leaving your car in the loading zone) to quickly pick them up.

2. **Book lessons far in advance.** They sell out.

3. **Brown bag it.** Our goal is to not set foot in a lodge for the entire holiday weekend (we use the bathrooms at the bottom of Roller Coaster or Chair 14 or, if desperate, in Little Eagle or McCoy Station, where the bathrooms are easier to get to than in Canyon and Main). Fighting for a table at Canyon on Martin Luther King Jr. weekend is not my idea of a fun vacation. Leave lunches in the car and meet for a tailgate party, or stash 'em in backpacks and meet at Outpost (the bottom of chairs 13 and 14), where picnic tables are usually plentiful. Best of all is if you can afford a ski-in, ski-out place— then you can ski back for lunch.

4. **Beat the crowds.** Be first on the chairs when they open at 8:30, take an early lunch break and ski from 12:30-2, while most folks are lunching. Quit by 3, to avoid that last-hour mob scene.

5. **Beware the shuttles.** Don't get me wrong—I love the Mammoth shuttle system and use it often. But I have also stood on Canyon Boulevard on Martin Luther King, Jr. weekend, watching seven jammed-full shuttles whiz by while I missed out on a lot of skiing. Sometimes the system gets overwhelmed on holidays, especially during the morning rush. (If you follow my advice and quit early, catching a shuttle home is a whole lot easier at 3 than at 4.) If you aren't lucky enough to have a ski-out or walking-distance condo, you might want to consider driving. My posse of friends and family usually drives to our secret place. (I'm sorry I can't tell you, but if you're clever you'll figure it out.) Alternatively, have a designated driver drop off your group at an easy spot (the Village gondola is fastest, followed by Little Eagle). Then the driver can park farther away and catch a shuttle. It's easier to fit one person on a crowded shuttle than a group.

6. **Be run-savvy.** See "Best Secret Runs," page 94.

How to make your kids **hate** skiing

→ First, start yelling at them to get their ski clothes on as soon as they wake up. Get breakfast in them as fast as possible, then hustle everyone out the door. Get angry when you realize that your 6-year-old dropped one of her gloves back in the condo. Stomp back to the condo and get it.

→ Try to get the kids to walk up the Canyon Lodge stairs faster than woolly mammoths. Roll your eyes when your 9-year-old says he has to go to the bathroom. Sigh deeply when he leans his snowboard against a wall near the bathroom and it falls, taking down six other snowboards with it.

→ Get them out on the snow. Help jam your six-year-old's boots into her bindings. "You're not pushing down hard enough," you snarl. Hustle her over to ski school and get her checked in fast, even though she says she's scared. Head over to Chair 17 to do some warm-up runs with the 9-year-old and your spouse.

→ When your 9-year-old announces that he's "starving" after two runs, remind him firmly that it's only 10:30 and it's nowhere near lunch, and besides, he didn't eat all of his breakfast like you told him. When he keeps asking, "When can we have lunch?" tell him if he asks one more time, you'll all be skipping lunch.

→ Pick up the 6-year-old from ski school at 1. Her teacher said she did great, but for some reason she's weepy. Head up to the Canyon cafeteria, which looks like rush hour in midtown Manhattan. Get visibly irritated when the people at the table you've staked out don't seem in any hurry to leave. When you finally get to sit, and your 6-year-old spills her cocoa, blurt out, "Damn it to hell!"

→ After lunch, when the kids say they're tired and want to quit, say, "I spent $155 just on lift tickets for us today, and we are not quitting!" Promise them you'll go sledding with them later if they ski longer.

→ When you quit at 3:30, yell at your daughter when she drops her skis on the floor in Canyon Lodge and refuses to pick them up, crying that her arms hurt. Tell the 9-year-old to hold it when he says he has to go to the bathroom. Get in a fight with your spouse about who's going to make the hike to get the car.

→ When you get back the condo, collapse in a heap. When the kids say it's time to go sledding, tell them you're just too tired and you'll do it tomorrow.

I hope you haven't had any days that bad, but as a veteran of mountain life with little kids, I can assure you that we all have our rough moments. Just hang around Canyon Lodge at 4 o'clock on any Saturday, and you'll see some mom or dad snapping at some exhausted kids. Skiing or boarding with young children demands a great deal of patience, money, patience, humor and patience. Here are the lessons I learned along the way:

→ **This was your idea.** Never forget that teaching your kids to ski or snowboard was your idea, not theirs. I've never heard of a 4-year-old who, out of blue, started begging to spend a whole day in ski school.

→ **Treat it as an investment.** Accept that much like the contribution to your 401K, family ski trips with small children are an investment in the future. Skiing and boarding are expensive. A family of four can easily spend $400 a day just on lessons, gear rental, lunch and lift tickets, and that's not counting the condo. There will be days, perhaps many of them, when you will not get $400 worth of enjoyment out of that investment. But in ten years, when you're ripping it up with your teenagers or young adult children, you'll reap the rewards of that investment.

→   **Take lots of breaks.** After years of pig-headedly refusing to stop to feed my kids before what I viewed as an acceptable lunchtime, I learned a valuable lesson from my friend Tom McHenry. He's the most gung-ho ski dad I've ever seen, capable of convincing scared 11-year-olds that they can ski Climax and getting them down it happily. One of his secrets is that the minute any kid in his charge says she's hungry or tired, he says, "Great! Let's go get a churro!" He knows that when their tanks are properly fueled and they get little rest breaks, kids won't melt down, whine or demand to quit.

→   **Plan to play.** Young children need to spend lots of time playing. It's how they experience the world, how they learn, how they express themselves. Skiing and snowboarding might be play for you, but it's not for them— it's a sport they are supposed to learn to make their parents happy. Play is making a snowman, building a snow fort, sledding, having a snowball fight, playing snow princesses. Eight hours of skiing, beer, dinner and bed is your idea of fun. So quit early and give them time for snow play, and get out there with them for a sled run or snowball fight.

→   **Avoid Saturday ski school.** Ski and snowboard school at Mammoth is usually packed on Saturdays. In my experience, the typical kid gets overwhelmed by a large class and often learns very little. Except on three-day weekends, Sunday ski school is less crowded, so take them yourself on Saturday and put them in school on Sunday. If you can stay for a non-holiday weekday, that's even better. If you want some instruction at Mammoth on Saturday or holiday weekends, consider the two-hour afternoon private lesson, for one to five kids. If you share the lesson with a couple of other kids, it's actually cheaper than putting them in ski school, and they'll get much more individual attention. Finally, if you have a nervous, shy or sensitive kid, and you really want them to be in ski school on a Saturday, consider going to less-crowded June Mountain for the day.

The **lingo**

Newcomers to Mammoth Mountain can sometimes feel like people who aren't being let into a secret society. Where is this "Chair 3" everybody keeps talking about? What are the "minarets"? Where is the mysterious "Warming Hut 2"? Here's a brief guide to the cryptic language used by old-timers, many of whom refuse to use the "new" names for many of the chairs and other mountain spots.

What old-timers call:	*Newcomers know as:*
The Backside:	**Chairs 13 and 14,** which are reached from the top of Chair 12. It doesn't necessarily look like a back side of the mountain—you'd think that would be behind Cornice—but it is.
Chair 1	Broadway Express
Chair 2	Stump Alley Express
Chair 3	Facelift Express
Chair 4	Roller Coaster
Chair 6	Thunder Bound
Chair 15	Little Eagle Express
The Grade	**Sherwin Grade,** otherwise known as the section of Highway 395 from Bishop to Mammoth
Lincoln Mountain	The smaller peak accessed by chairs 22 and 25
Mid-Chalet	McCoy Station
The Minarets	The dramatic granite spires northwest of Mammoth, visible from many upper chairlifts and runs
Warming Hut 2	Canyon Lodge

Renting & servicing **gear**

Renting gear

Rental places abound; where to go depends on your situation.

If you live in Southern California and want to rent basic ski or snowboard packages, one of the best and least-stressful deals is found at **Sport Chalet.** The ski/boot/pole package is $30 for the first day and $5 for each subsequent day; they don't charge for the day you pick up and the day you return. Kids' gear is $18 the first day and $4 for extra days. Snowboard packages cost a little more. For a several-day trip, the low subsequent-day charge makes this the most affordable option, plus you don't have to deal with renting gear when you arrive, when setting up house is enough work. Sport Chalet rental shops are found at its branches in La Canada, Irvine, Porter Ranch, Torrance, San Diego (the Midway Drive location) and Rancho Cucamonga. The equipment here is well maintained and fine for beginners to intermediates, but you won't find higher-quality demo gear.

If you're a Val, another good place to rent gear is at **Val Surf,** which has locations in North Hollywood, Woodland Hills, Thousand Oaks and Valencia. Its ski packages are a better deal than Sport Chalet: $18 for one day, $30 for two and $38 for three. For snowboard packages, you'll pay $30 for one day, $45 for two and $55 for three. If you pick up after 1 p.m. and return before 1 p.m., there's no charge for those days. Higher-quality performance gear is available at a cost.

Many people, however, prefer to wait until they get to the mountain to get their gear. Sometimes they have fit problems and want to be able to swap out boots. Sometimes they're demoing higher-end gear. Sometimes they don't have room in the car to fit the gear. And sometimes they just run out of time. Here's a roster of the best places to rent ski and snowboard gear in town; allow an hour or so to get outfitted before you hit the mountain.

Command Performance

26 Old Mammoth Rd., Mammoth
(760) 934-4447, 800-FASTSKI

A small, friendly spot that will let you reserve gear in advance, this place is also called Fastski, thanks to its selection of racing and high-end demo skis. A basic ski package is $28 a day and $54 for two days; kids rent free with adult rentals. Racing skis, of course, cost more.

Footloose

Main St. & Old Mammoth Rd., Mammoth
www.footloosesports.com
(760) 934-2400

If you're looking to rent higher-end demo gear at a better price than on the mountain, head for Footloose. It has quality equipment, friendly people and good service. The folks here are famous for their bootfitting, so if you need boots and have foot issues, come here. A basic ski or snowboard package is$25 a day ($16 for kids); a demo ski package is $35. Discounts are offered for longer-term rentals.

Mammoth Mountain

Basic rental reservations: (800) MAMMOTH
www.mammothmountain.com

During uncrowded times, renting on the mountain is the most convenient, though not the most economical. Locations are found at Canyon Lodge, Main Lodge, Little Eagle and the new Mountain Center next to the Village gondola. Entry-level ski packages are $27 a day, sport-ski packages are $33, and snowboard packages are $30; kids pay $17 for basic ski or snowboard packages. There are no subsequent-day discounts.

On the Edge Performance Centers

Main Lodge, 2nd floor, (760) 934-0670
Canyon Lodge, 2nd floor, (760) 934-0770
Mountain Center, lower level, the Village, (760) 924-7057
Little Eagle Lodge, (760) 934-2571, ext. 3417
www.mammothmountain.com/ski_ride/rental_demo/demo

These are the higher-end performance-equipment centers on the mountain. The Main and Canyon branches are the easiest way to demo new equipment, because you can stop back in as many times as you like during the day to swap out gear. If you land up buying new boots or boards, part of your rental cost will be applied toward the purchase. Demo rates vary; skis alone, for example, are $45, a ski package is $59, and a demo snowboard package is $49. Multi-day discounts are available, except during holidays.

Rick's Sport Center
3241 Main St., Mammoth
(760) 934-3416

With a two-day ski package running just $26 for two days ($20 for kids), Rick's is the best deal in town. Snowboard packages are $20 for the first day. There's a limited selection of higher-end demo gear. Take note that in the second week of April, Rick's closes down its rental operation to become a fishing store.

Wave Rave
3203 Main St., Mammoth
(760) 934-2471

The best snowboard shop in town, for rentals, service and sales, is owned by snowboard legend Steve Klassen. A basic board package is $25 a day; demos are also available.

Servicing Gear

For ski and snowboard tune-ups and repairs, a good bet in Mammoth is the **Ski Surgeon** (6085 Minaret Rd., 760-934-6370), located next to the Village gondola. Other good places are **Footloose** and **Kittredge** (3218 Main St., 760-934-7566). Mammoth Mountain's **On the Edge** repair shops at Canyon and Main are also reliable. For snowboard tune-ups and repairs, go to **Wave Rave.** For tele, Nordic, mountaineering and climbing gear, go to **Mammoth Mountaineering Supply** (3189 Main Street, 760-934-4191). **Command Performance** offers free ski hot waxing and excellent overnight ski tuning.

Should I buy
a **season pass?**

For me, that's like asking if I should buy food to eat. The Mammoth Value Pass (MVP), typically offered in limited numbers on April 1, is so valued by regulars that we start hitting the speed dial button the second they go on sale. For $425 ($319 for teens, $213 for kids and seniors), you get unlimited skiing and boarding at Mammoth and June from May 1 of the preceding season through the entire fol-lowing season, plus free scenic gondola rides in summer, 50% off lift tickets at other Intrawest resorts, a 10% discount at all mountain shops and midweek discounts on everything from lessons to lodging. After your seventh day on the mountain, you're skiing free for the rest of the season...and you cannot underestimate the lifting of Skier's Guilt that the pass brings. Let's say it's a holiday-weekend Monday and the kids have to be home by 6 because of homework, but you'd really like to get in a few runs. Pay $62 for a lift ticket for 90 minutes of boarding?! No way! But if you have a pass, you just head up for a few happy, guilt-free runs. Quit early? No guilt problems with a pass. Stay in on a stormy day? No problem with a pass.

That said, passes aren't for everyone. If you won't ski at least seven days at Mammoth or June, it's not worth it. If you ski a lot but do one Mammoth trip and other trips to other mountains, it's not worth it—and if you're not a skier, of course, it's a waste of money.

If you decide an MVP is for you, call (800) MAMMOTH or go to www.mammoth-mtn.com no later than April 1 of the preceding ski season to learn how to buy a pass.

If you're a mountain biker who spends lots of summer time in Mammoth, take note that there's a Mammoth Bike Park pass, too.

Note to spouses, employers and loved ones: An MVP makes a fabulous gift for any Mammoth regular. Just ask my sister Cammie, my brother Michael and me. Thanks, Mom and Dad, for our annual birthday present!

Ski school
dos & don'ts

→   **Do:** Make reservations for group or private lessons at Mammoth the moment you commit to your trip. Lessons are often fully booked for weekends, and for holidays they book up many weeks in advance. Call (800) MAMMOTH.

→   **Don't:** Assume all instructors are the same. They can be just as inattentive, arrogant, or boring as anyone else. Ask your friends for recommendations. My family and friends have a few favorites, but they're popular, so book them very, very early. Our favorite ski instructors for kids are **Patti O'Donnell Dawley** and **Cath Moran**, both of whom are warm, wise, incredibly personable and positive. For teens and adults, our favorite ski instructor is **Ian Sinclair**, who has the little-seen level-three certification; he made a huge difference for my young teenager. Cath Moran's husband, **Anthony Horn**, is also a good ski instructor for teenagers and adults. Snowboarders of any age should try to get **Brent Collins**. If you're a skier looking to try snowboarding, book a lesson with **Gary Paolino**, who specializes in linking the two skills. All of these instructors can be booked by calling Mammoth's main reservation number, (800) MAMMOTH.

→   **Do:** Share an afternoon private lesson. The two-hour sessions are $130 ($140 on Saturdays), and you can have up to five people. This is particularly recommended for kids, who will get much more attention than in a group lesson, even if you fill up all five slots. But it's great for adults, too. And if you share the lesson, it's cheaper per person than if you each went to ski school.

→   **Don't:** Put kids in a Saturday-morning or holiday-season group lesson if you can help it. At Mammoth, they're typically too crowded.

→   **Do:** Consider June. It's less crowded on all fronts, including in ski/snowboard school.

→   **Don't:** Think you're too good for lessons. An early-bird private lesson, from 8:45 to 9:45 a.m., can do wonders to kick your skiing or boarding up a notch, even if you're already a ripper.

Why **June?**

Some people prefer Hondas, some Chevys. You say "tomato," I say "tomahto." So it goes with the preference for either Mammoth or June. True, June can't begin to compare with Mammoth in terms of sheer size and diversity of terrain. But it has its charms and its diehard fans. Here are six reasons to ski or board June Mountain:

1. **It's a Saturday.** Almost every Saturday in season is busy at Mammoth, and the holiday Saturdays can be insane. Meanwhile, over at June, every other chair is empty—even the pokey old two-person chairs.

2. **You're a Beginner.** Mammoth has first-rate instructors and plenty of beginner terrain, but June wins out for beginners because of its broad, open, often-empty runs. It's a lot easier to relax and learn the sport when there aren't two dozen snowboarders barreling down right behind you. June's terrain is, on average, gentler than Mammoth's, with 80% labeled beginner or intermediate terrain.

3. **You Have Little Kids.** Because it is relatively small, it's easier for kids to get the lay of the land at June. Most children like to practice the same run over and over and over, so getting bored isn't an issue for them. (Parents are another matter.) And because the rating scale is more generous than at Mammoth, your little hot-dogger can go back to school boasting about ripping up a "black diamond" run. He doesn't need to know that it'd be a blue run at Mammoth.

4. **You Want Terrain-Park Action.** Mammoth has terrain parks galore, but June has surprisingly good ones that are generally less crowded and lots of fun. There's also a good learning area with mini-rails just a few inches off the snow base, so you can try grinding a rail without necessarily breaking a bone.

5. **There's Fresh Snow.** Huge as Mammoth is, its best freshies can get tracked up in seemingly minutes. June's powder is known for lasting longer, mostly because it just gets less people. Powder junkies head straight for the face, which looms over the parking lot and the runs off the J7 chair.

6. **You're on a Budget.** If you've already bought a Mammoth lift ticket or season pass, both of which are good at June, this won't apply. But if you haven't, June is a better deal. The 2003-2004 ticket prices were $50 a day and $88 for two days, or just $44 a day. That compares to Mammoth's $62

weekend rate, with a puny two-day discount (and no two-day discount for holidays). Ski/board school, rentals and private lessons are a little cheaper, too.

June Mountain facts

June is located on Highway 158 just west of Highway 395, twenty miles north of Mammoth. If you're staying in Mammoth, it's a bit faster to take the Mammoth Scenic Loop shortcut to the 395 instead of heading back through town. You'll pass June Lake and its fetching little village, then come upon a large (free!) parking lot. If you're a beginner or have nervous kids, don't panic at the sight of the steep mogul runs, the only runs you can see from the parking lot. The chair at the base, J1, ferries people up to the heart of the mountain, where you'll find four other chairs leading to lots of gentle terrain.

The town is sleepy—after a recent Saturday of June skiing, we planned to stop in town for refreshments, but everything—the coffee-house, the ice-cream shop, the pizza parlor—was closed up tight for the afternoon. But it's cute as a button and has affordable cabins and clean budget motels.

Enjoy this sleepiness while you can...Intrawest is coming. Plans are afoot to replace creaky chair J1 with a gondola and build a honkin' big 90-acre, 800-bed development (the current town has only 600 residents!) across from the parking lot. It doesn't have a permit at this writing, and June Lake Advocates are fighting it, but Intrawest tends to get what it wants, so many locals are worried.

June and Mammoth are partners, so your Mammoth ticket is good at June—but because they're cheaper, your June ticket is not good at Mammoth.

For information on lift tickets, ski/board school and more, go to www.junemountain.com, or call (888) JUNEMTN.

Wind is your **friend**

It took me a long time to understand this maxim, which is often quoted by old-timers. Mammoth is known for its wind, which often batters the top at 60, 70, 80 miles per hour. When it really starts blowing, the highest chairs and the upper gondola shut down, and lots of fair-weather skiers and boarders head inside. You can't blame them, especially if you've just ridden the Canyon Express chair with an ice-flecked wind blowing up your nose and into the seams of your thickest gloves.

But here's what that wind does: It blows the snow into lots of swell places, collecting in smooth yet fluffy caches all around the mountain. Wind-buffed Mammoth snow is well worth the personal torture of negotiating, say, the top of Scotty's, with gusts blowing so hard that I've seen children blown right back off the edge. But once you drop below the howling, swirling top of such advanced runs as Scotty's, Dave's and Climax, and such intermediate runs as Back for More and St. Anton, the gusts diminish and you get to sail through soft, light, heavenly snow.

And because all the lightweights are sitting by their fireplaces with hot toddies (not such a bad fate either), you'll have few people to compete with for that wind-buffed white stuff.

SIERRA FUN:
SUMMERTIME, WINTERTIME, ANYTIME

The sky is mostly sunshine, oftentimes tempered by magnificent clouds, the breath of the sea built up into new mountain ranges, warm during the day, cool at night, good flower opening weather.
— John Muir, *Our National Parks*

The aging process has you firmly in its grasp if you never get the urge to throw a snowball.
— Doug Larson

Skiing, boarding, hiking and fishing aren't the only ways to have fun in the Eastern Sierra. The pages that follow will inspire you to do so much more: sled, rock climb, kayak, get a massage, attend a music festival, ice skate, soak in a hot springs, follow a guide into the backcountry, snowshoe and even play golf.

Winterfun

CROSS-COUNTRY SKIING

Both free and pay trails wind through the Mammoth area and up into the higher elevations at Rock Creek Lake. The listings below will steer you in the right direction. If you need to rent cross-country gear, go to either Mammoth Mountaineering Supply (see "Shops Worth Knowing About," page 147) or Tamarack, next page.

Inyo Craters Trail
Mammoth Scenic Loop Rd., 3.5 miles north of Mammoth

Look for the Inyo Craters sign on the Mammoth Scenic Loop and you'll see a wide trail heading into the woods. (You might see other cars and skiers, too—it's a popular spot.) This is a lovely eight-kilometer route, mostly easy with a couple of mildly challenging spots.

Mammoth Town Trails
Mammoth Lakes Visitor Center and Ranger Station
Hwy. 203 (Main St.), Mammoth
(760) 924-5500
www.fs.fed.us/r5/inyo/vc/mammoth.html

The town of Mammoth Lakes maintains a number of free Nordic trails, most of which start at this Forest Service visitor's center. The trails are generally easy and well defined. If you need directions or guidance, a ranger at the visitor's center will help you.

Rock Creek Lodge
Rock Creek Rd., 8 miles up from Tom's Place
(877) 935-4170
www.rockcreeklodge.com

For a cross-country experience you'll not soon forget, book an overnight stay at this rustic High Sierra lodge not far from Rock Creek Lake. They'll pick you up in a snowmobile further down Rock Creek Road and take you to the small lodge and collection of cabins. Here you'll find fifteen miles of groomed cross-country trails, through open meadows and quiet forests, with snow-covered peaks overhead. And because of the high elevation (almost 10,000 feet), the snow is light and fluffy, not the Sierra cement you see at 7,000 feet.

The lodge will set you up with whatever you need: lessons, a guide and gear; they even have Nordic ski gear for little kids. And at the end of the day, you can bake in the Finnish sauna, then join the other guests for a hot, hearty dinner around the family-style table.

For details on staying overnight at the lodge, see the review on page 48.

Tamarack Cross Country Ski Center

Twin Lakes Loop Rd., off Lake Mary Rd., Mammoth
(760) 934-5293
Open mid-Nov.–mid-April, depending on snowfall

This first-rate Nordic ski center is the hub of 45 kilometers of groomed trails, ranging from the short and easy to the long and more challenging. You can ski around Lake Mary, or over to Lake George, or through pine forests, or around Panorama Dome; all trails are far from cars and other signs of modern life. Snowshoes, dogs, sleds and such are not allowed on the Nordic trails, but there are a few trails set aside especially for snowshoers and walkers.

Tamarack offers rentals and group and private lessons, for both adults and children; it also organizes races and fun Nordic events. Trail passes, lessons and rentals are reasonably priced. An adult trail pass is $19 a day ($22 on Saturdays), with half-day and twilight rates offered; kids 9 and under ski free. Beginners can get set up with gear, trail pass and lessons for $55 ($59 on Saturdays), less for kids, seniors and afternoon sessions.

At the end of your session, stop in the lodge and recover from all that fresh air with a cocoa or a chardonnay next to the fireplace.

GUIDED BACKCOUNTRY SKIING
& ICE CLIMBING

See "Guided Climbing & Hiking" under Summer Fun, page 122.

ICE SKATING

Mammoth Lakes Ice Rink

Hwy. 203 and Sierra Park Rd. (next to Mammoth Community Church), Mammoth
(760) 924-7733

Open mid-Nov.–mid-March for public skating daily 11:30 a.m.–2:30 p.m.
*   and 3–6 p.m. (Fri.–Sat. to 9:30 p.m.)*
Adults $7, children $5, 4 and under free; rentals $3 for adults and children,
* $2 kids 4 & under*

It's not the most beautiful setting in the world, in a rather scrubby meadow next to a church, but the mountain views are great, and you'll get plenty of invigorating mountain air while you skate. The center offers rentals, figure-skating lessons, pick-up hockey games (call for times), modest snacks and drinks and, on special nights, campfires. Friday night is family night, when just $3 gets you a skate session and rental skates.

SLEDDING

Suitable sledding hills can be found all over Mammoth and the Eastern Sierra—just keep your eyes peeled for a good pitch and an open stretch. My kids' favorite spot is actually a hole in the ground in the woods just off the bottom of the Roller Coaster chair and Chair 20; we often end a ski day with a sled session into this pit, with forays to a nearby graded road. Another favorite sledding spot of Mammoth kids is, sadly, about to become another housing development. But look and you will find other sled hills throughout Mammoth, June and the surrounding country.

In addition to seeking out free sled hills, you can shell out money to innertube at the place that follows.

Sledz

Minaret Rd., en route to Main Lodge, Mammoth
(760) 934-7533

Open daily in winter 10 a.m.–4 p.m.
$10 per hour per person

My kids love this place, and I have to admit, I've had a lot of fun here, too. For ten bucks an hour, you can grab a fat innertube, let the rope tow haul you up 500 feet, come careening down the run, and do it all over again. It's most fun to double up on a big innertube. When it gets icy, especially in spring, this can be a pretty hairy ride—little kids can go flying off the inner-tubes when they start bouncing on the icy ruts. But they're usually laughing all the way. Take note that this place seems to be permanently for sale, so ownership, hours, prices and everything could change at any moment.

SNOWMOBILING & DOG SLEDDING

DJ's Snowmobile Adventures

Staging area 1: Hwy. 395, 3 miles north of Hwy. 203
Staging area 2: Mammoth Scenic Loop Rd., off Minaret Rd., Mammoth
(760) 935-4480
www.snowmobilemammoth.com

1-hr. rides $60 ($78 for 2 riders), 2-hr. $104, 3-hr. $156

A long-established snowmobile business, DJ's has a fleet of machines that can be seen all winter long on the edge of a huge meadow on Highway 395 just north of Mammoth. This is a good place to come if you want to give it a try—a family or friends can take turns on a snowmobile in the open meadow area for $60 a hour. Or you can rent your own and follow the map printed right on your snowmobile to marked trails through the meadows and woods in this open country. If you want to really explore, consider a guided tour. Experienced snowmobilers can take a thrilling steep trail up around Indiana Summit.

Dog Sled Adventures
Main Lodge, Mammoth
(760) 934-6270

Rides $39–$65 adults, $19–$28 children 12 and under, free for children under 3

If you've skied or boarded in the Main Lodge area, you've probably seen these teams of huskies. And if you've had kids with you, they've probably begged you to take them on a ride. And there's absolutely no reason why you shouldn't—these dogs are clearly well cared for, and they love charging through the snow. You can choose from a 25-minute loop through the forest just beyond the ski area or a one-hour ride that goes farther into the back-country. Or ditch the kids and take the two-person Wintermoon trip, which includes dinner at the Mammoth Mountain Inn, champagne and a 45-minute moonlight sled ride.

Mammoth Snowmobile Adventures
Main Lodge, Mammoth
(760) 934-9645, (800) MAMMOTH
www.mammoth-mtn.com/activities/snomo

Tours $50 (1-hr.) to $275 (all day)

Okay, so it's not as peaceful and environmentally correct as Nordic and alpine skiing—but snowmobiling with this outfit sure is fun. The one-hour ride, through trees and small meadows, is fine, but I'd recommend splurging on the two-hour tour—you get to see more of Mammoth's backcountry, and you'll get to really open it up (and maybe even jump a little). The guides/instructors are good people, and they'll make sure you have a good time. Two-person snowmobiles are also available, a popular choice for families (kids as young as 5 can ride with an adult). This is the best snowmobiling operation in the area.

SNOWSHOEING

You can snowshoe anywhere your legs will take you in the Eastern Sierra, although you'll find it easier going on roads instead of through forests, where snow drifts can be thick and tough to get through. You'll find great snowshoe routes at Tamarack's cross-country center (see "Cross-country Skiing," page 117), and there are some good roads behind Mammoth's visitor's center, too, as well as around the town.

If you need to rent snowshoes, head for Tamarack (see page 117) or Mammoth Mountaineering Supply (see page 147).

Summerfun

CLIMBING & ROPES COURSES

The Body Shop Sports Training
3059 Chateau Rd., Mammoth
(760) 934-3700

Open Mon.–Fri. 6 a.m.–9 p.m., Sat.–Sun. 8 a.m.–8 p.m.
Day rates not yet established

This large, snazzy new gym opened just as the book was going to press, so I didn't have time to check it out in person. But club owners Matt and Tina Graeff are proud of the new climbing wall, a $75,000 wall created by Entre Prises. If you're a climbing-wall buff, make sure to give this one a try.

Mammoth Climb 'n' Zip
Mammoth Adventure Center, Main Lodge, Mammoth
(760) 934-0706, (800) MAMMOTH

Open June–Sept. daily 9 a.m.–5 p.m.
Single climb or zip $9, 1-hr. climb $19, junior ropes course $19, private lesson $25

The centerpiece of this place between Main Lodge and the Mammoth Mountain Inn is the 35-foot-high climbing wall, on which a dozen or so routes range from the easy to the scary (scary for novices, that is). Don't waste the $9 on a single climb—you'll want another one in short order, and it can get expensive fast. Instead, get the $19 one-hour session, which you can share with friends. (I bought the one-hour session for three teenagers, who had a blast and got plenty of climbing in during the one hour.) The wall is open to climbers of all ages; most are between 5 and 25, but over-50s have fun on it, too.

Next to the climbing wall is a 110-foot zip line and a modest junior ropes course; both are open only to kids 13 and under. They're great fun and highly recommended.

GUIDED CLIMBING & HIKING

Experienced climbers who don't need or want guides have some of the best climbs in the country to enjoy. See the climbing-related books in Chapter 13, "Essential Resources," for advice on where to go. Even more climbing guidebooks and maps can be found at the region's outdoors stores, especially Wilson's in Bishop and Mammoth Mountaineering in Mammoth.

Sierra Mountain Center

174 W. Line St., Bishop
(760) 873-8526
www.sierramountaincenter.com

Probably the largest guide and training operation in the Eastern Sierra, this outfit has it all: classes in avalanche training and backcountry ski touring; spring corn-skiing camps; parent-child snow outings and climbing/moun-tain-exploring weekends; rock-climbing lessons; alpine ice climbs for begin-ners to experts; two- to seven-day ski tours; fourteeners camps; Mt. Whitney climbs; and mountaineering trips (dubbed the Freezing Your Ass Off Series). The highly experienced instructors and guides also train would-be instructors in classes certified by the American Mountain Guides Association. If you can snag an outing with Howie Schwartz, do it—he's one of the best guides in the business, whether you're looking for an ice climb, a ski tour or a classic mountain climb. (Schwartz also has his own website, www.alpineguide.net.)

If you're a downhill skier ready for a backcountry challenge, one of the guides will take you to an untracked bowl for some safe (meaning low ava-lanche risk) fresh-powder action. It's not helicopter skiing—you'll have to do some hiking—but it's a thrill nonetheless.

Sierra Mountaineering International

236 N. Main St., Bishop
(760) 872-4929
www.sierramountaineering.com

Founded and run by accomplished mountaineer Kurt Wedberg, this outfit is known for its avalanche, rock-climbing and mountaineering classes, its back-country skiing and boarding classes and its guided climbs up many Eastern Sierra peaks, including Whitney. Most extraordinary is its once-a-year, eight-day spring ski tour traversing the top of the Sierra from east to west, finishing in the giant Sequoias; at the end of the eight days, a chartered plane picks you up and flies you back, right over the route you just skied. Wedberg and his fellow guides also lead private climbs.

HORSEBACK RIDING & PACK TRIPS

Stables are found throughout the Eastern Sierra; some offer short horseback rides, which can be great fun, and others specialize in multi-day pack trips. Packing in by horse or mule has several advantages: It can bring physically limited or frail people into the High Sierra; it provides easier access to remote areas; it makes longer-term backcountry trips more feasible; and it can be a wonderful way for multi-generational families to have a backcountry adventure together.

That said, be aware that the Eastern Sierra's many pack outfitters have their critics, including a number of Forest Service rangers. The critics say that so many horses and mules overwhelm the trail system, trampling flora and leaving a lot of animal waste behind. And they complain that many pack outfitters don't do enough to maintain the trails, almost all of which are shared with hikers. On the other hand, all packers pay fees to use the backcountry, which helps replenish desperately thin Forest Service funds.

So by all means enjoy a pack adventure, but consider asking prospective pack outfits how they maintain trails and minimize the environmental impact of their trips. It helps them to know that people care. Also, consider hiking instead of riding—a few pack mules carrying gear is less intrusive than adding an extra horse per person.

Mammoth Lakes Pack Outfit
Lake Mary Rd., 4 miles from central Mammoth
(760) 934-2434, (888) 475-8747
www.mammothpack.com

1-hr. trip $35, 2-hr. trips $60, half-day trips $80

Although it offers backcountry pack trips, this large stable is really more of a day-ride outfit, with a particular focus on families. It has a lot of kind, well-cared-for horses and a staff of congenial riders. Some of the easygoing horseback rides are fun for kids 7 and up, including the one-hour trip up Panorama Dome and the 90-minute trip to Mammoth Consolidated Mine. Kids age 9 and up are welcome on the two-hour trips; consider the one to lovely Emerald Lake. (Really little ones can do the half-hour "walk and lead" ride around the stables.) If you're up for a big adventure, try the all-day trip to Barney Lake; it provides plenty of time to hike, fish or fool around.

McGee Creek Pack Station
Off Hwy. 395, 30 miles north of Bishop, Crowley Lake
(760) 935-4324
www.mcgeecreekpackstation.com

A long-established, highly regarded pack outfitter, McGee Creek is also known for its efforts to maintain the trail system. It offers a roster of day rides (the half-day ride up McGee Canyon is fabulous and a bargain at $60), but the real specialty is backcountry trips into the high mountain country around McGee Creek, or to Convict Basin or Upper Fish Creek. You can hike or ride to a base camp, where pack mules will deliver your gear and come back to get you a few days later; consider choosing Dorothy Lake in Convict Basin as your home base. Or you can move from camp to camp, keeping the pack team with you while you explore many High Sierra lakes, creeks, meadows and peaks. A well-run outfit that will ensure a memorable pack trip—or day ride—McGee Creek is also a well-run lodge resort, with nine comfortable, inexpensive rooms and a restaurant.

Red's Meadow Pack Outfitters

End of Hwy. 203, past Devil's Postpile, Mammoth
(760) 934-2345, (800) 292-7758
www.reds-meadow.com

Run by Bob Tanner for 45 years (and a pack outfit for 25 years before that), this large, successful operation is now for sale. The Tanners are looking to retire, so by the time you read this, the operation could be different—although with its history, one would expect new buyers to carry on as ever.

Located on the edge of Red's Meadow, where Highway 203 ends past Mammoth, this cabin resort/general store/café/pack outfit has an ideal spot for Sierra access. You can book all sorts of private outings, from a dunnage trip, where your gear and food are delivered by pack to a particular spot, to which you hike, to an all-inclusive custom trip complete with guide and cook. More economical are the scheduled group trips, which take place throughout the summer. These include four-day parent-child rides to a gorgeous six-day ride from Red's Meadow to Tuolomne Meadow in Yosemite.

Or, if you have a *City Slickers* fantasy, you can spend $645 and join in on the annual three-day spring or fall horse drives, when the horses and mules are moved to and from the high country for the season.

Rock Creek Pack Station

Rock Creek Rd., 10 miles up from Tom's Place
(760) 872-8331
www.rockcreekpackstation.com

The best of the Sierra can be accessed with these equestrians, whose pack station is just above Rock Creek Lake. No one-hour trail rides here: Outings range from overnighters to two-week-long backcountry adventures. Craig and Herbert London will tailor the outing to your liking. Some opt for a spot trip, where horses and pack mules deliver you and your stuff to a remote campsite, say past Mono Pass, and return to pick you up on a date of your choice. Others prefer the organized group trail rides to such beautiful spots as Hilton Lakes (you can either ride or hike, with pack mules hauling the gear). The deep of pocket go for the all-expense trips, which typically include a cook, a fishing guide and top-notch gear and food. Families take note of the popular three-day guided parent-child trail ride, offered several times during the summer.

IF YOU MUST GOLF

I'm no golfer, but if I was, I'd be happy to play at the courses below—they're so beautiful that instead of getting angry every time I sliced the ball, I could look heavenward at the Sierras and feel peaceful.

Bishop Country Club
Hwy. 395, Bishop
(760) 873-5828

Open year-round; greens fees for 18 holes $40 Mon.–Thurs., $45 weekends and holidays, $27 for seniors, $15 for juniors; discounts for twilight play and 9 holes; cart rental $15

On one side are soaring Sierra peaks; on the other are the looming White Mountains. This is a wonderful (and good value) 18-hole public course, rich in natural and man-made beauty, with water on most holes, stately trees and lush greens. It's a fairly flat course, with room for nice, long drives—but lest you think the flatness will make for an easy day's golf, remember the many water hazards. This course is particularly lovely in fall, when some of the leaves change color. Unlike at the Mammoth courses, you can play year-round here, but be warned that morning tee times can get delayed due to frost.

The facilities are complete: pro shop, driving range, restaurant, bar, cart and club rentals and lessons.

Sierra Star
2001 Sierra Star Pkwy., Mammoth
(760) 924-GOLF, (800) MAMMOTH
www.mammothmountain.com

Open late May–mid-Oct.; greens fees for 18 holes $95 weekdays, $115 weekends, $50 for juniors; discounts for twilight play

This par-70, 18-hole golf course in the heart of Mammoth is the highest in California, at 8,000 feet. Designed by Newport Beach's Cal Olsen, it is also considered one of the most challenging courses in the state, so come with modest performance expectations. On the one hand, golf balls soar farther at this altitude; on the other, this is a tight course, winding through thick pine forests, so precision is more important than power. But the course's short length makes it a little more forgiving, so more novice golfers shouldn't get too frustrated.

Besides the 18-hole course—the only one in Mammoth—the facility includes a pro shop, putting and chipping green, swing nets, a café and a bar.

Greens fees include a cart, but if you'd rather walk—a great idea in this beautiful spot—they'll give you a pull cart.

Snowcreek Golf Course

Old Mammoth Rd. and Fairway Dr., Mammoth
(760) 934-6633
www.snowcreekresort.com

Open late May–Oct. 31; greens fees for 9 holes $30, $27 for seniors and kids 17
and under, $18 for Snowcreek renters; electric and pull carts extra

Designed by Ted Robinson and built in 1990, this 9-hole, par-35 course sits in the middle of Mammoth Meadows, with mountain views all around. It has water hazards on seven of the holes, so accuracy is important; the elevated greens are known for being particularly fast.

Pro Rich Voss organizes fun tournaments and events throughout the summer, and he and his staff are known for their teaching ability. Other on-site amenities include a driving range, pro shop, café and rentals. Go for the pull cart—this is a lovely place to walk.

By the way, Snowcreek has been trying for some time to work out a deal with the Forest Service to expand to 18 holes, but it's had no luck yet.

MOUNTAIN BIKING

Fantastic bike trails snake throughout the Eastern Sierra, and other than the ones on Mammoth Mountain, which are controlled by the Mammoth Mountain Bike Park (see page 128), they're all free. Many are marked and/or mapped routes, but you can also just head off down any of the seemingly endless dirt roads in the region.

I have neither the space nor the mapping capabilities to properly point you to the best rides in the area. Instead, stop at any local outdoors store and buy the **Eastern High Sierra Recreation Topo Map** (Fine Edge Productions, $8.95). Covering the area from Crowley Lake to Mono Lake, this map is extremely clear, with lots of bike-friendly routes ranging from single-track to dirt roads, and it also shows which areas are off-limits to bicycles. The map also details many area hiking trails. You should also pick up the new edition of ***Mountain Biking The***

Eastern Sierra's Best 100 Trails (Mountain Biking Press, $18.95), an essential resource for cyclists.

Renting Bikes

Other than at **Mammoth Mountain Bike Park** (see below), the best place in Mammoth to rent bikes is **Mammoth Sporting Goods** (Sierra Center Mall, Old Mammoth Road, 760-934-3239). It has a good selection for all sizes, including bikes for little kids; tandems, helmets and baby trailers are also available. Rates are $8 an hour for a basic bike and $10 for a full-suspension model, with half-day rates at $24 and $30, respectively. Demo bikes are $45 a half-day and $60 all day. Look for the yellow flyers around town, which will give you a 25-percent discount. The nice people here will give you advice and provide you with a good map of the bike trails around Mammoth, ranging from flat cruisers to serious single-track.

Bike Park

Mammoth Mountain Bike Park

Mammoth Adventure Center
Main Lodge, Minaret Rd., Mammoth
(760) 934-0706, (800) MAMMOTH
www.mammothmountain.com

Open daily in summer 9 a.m.–4:30 p.m.
1-day trail-only pass $10 adults, $5 kids; 1-day full pass (includes gondola and shuttle)
    $31 adults, $16 kids; half-day pass with bike rental $50 adults, $25 kids;
    various combinations of passes and rentals available

If you think bungee jumping isn't quite scary enough, put a bike on the gondola and ride to the top of Mammoth Mountain, then try to make it down one of the expert bike runs—they are steep, terrifying and covered with sharp pumice-rock scree instead of forgiving snow. But you don't have to be a thrill-seeker to enjoy riding here—the bike park has 80 miles of maintained single-track ranging from the most challenging to the quite easy. The most popular easy routes are Paper Route, a long, fun course that loops all the way to Little Eagle and back, and Downtown, a gentle downhill that takes you through tall-pine forest to the Village. From the Village, you can cycle back on Uptown, a moderate uphill trail through the same forest, or wimp out and catch the Adventure Center's shuttle, which will bring you and your bike back to Main Lodge.

If you're planning on riding the rocky stuff, rent one of the bike park's bikes instead of using your own, unless you have a super-fat-tire bike with a first-rate suspension system, and you don't mind giving it a beating. The rental rates are quite reasonable when combined with a pass.

ON THE LAKES

The Eastern Sierra has more lakes than you can shake a fishing pole at. The majority can be reached only on foot or by horseback (see Chapter 8, "Twelve Great Hikes," and the section on horseback riding on page 123 for how to reach a few). But the lakes covered in this section all have marinas, boat rentals and such extras as fishing tackle. Note that only June Lake has beaches set aside just for swimming; you can swim in any lake, but you might not want to in most, unless you want a fish hook in your backside. For lake-fishing details, see Chapter 9, "Gone Fishing."

Caldera Kayaks
Crowley Lake Marina, Crowley Lake
(760) 935-4942
www.calderakayak.com

Caldera is based at Crowley Lake, but it will rent you kayaks (and car racks) to take anywhere you like—and the nice folks there will steer you toward good lakes for kayaking. These folks are also known for their excellent tours of Mono Lake—and kayaking is by far the best way to experience the beauty and wonder of Mono. Caldera also offers group and private lessons (including lessons for kids) at Crowley, as well as guided tours of that lake.

Convict Lake

Convict Lake Resort
Rte. 1, off Hwy. 395, just south of Mammoth Airport
(760) 934-3800

Paddleboats $16 for 1 hr.
Rowboats, kayaks and canoes $12 for 1 hr., $25 half-day
Motorboats $16 for 1 hr., $50 half-day;
Pontoon boats $45 for 1 hr.

Few local lakes pack more dramatic punch than Convict—the granite walls of Laurel Mountain and Mount Morrison plunge almost straight into the lake. It's a wonderful place to fish, paddle a kayak or hike around the shore. The little marina rents boats at reasonable rates; the excellent general store has all sorts of fishing supplies. Serious fishermen love the challenge of this lake—its ultra-clear waters make catching a trout tough, but it's stocked regularly, so they're in there!

Crowley Lake

Crowley Lake Fish Camp
Landing Rd., off Hwy. 395, Crowley Lake
(760) 935-4301

Motorboats $50–$65 for half-day, $60–$75 all day
Pontoon boats $150 for half-day
For kayaks see Caldera Kayaks page 129

This is quite a large marina by Eastern Sierra standards, but then Crowley is a large lake, with 45 miles of shoreline and 650 acres of water. Fishing is the name of the game here: On the season's opening day each April, fishermen come from far and wide for the Big Fish contest and general festivities, and throughout the season, Crowley is frequently restocked with trout. The lake is not a "typical" Eastern Sierra lake—those lakes are often ringed with forest and overseen by dramatic peaks, while Crowley sits on the broad, flat Long Valley Caldera plain, surrounded by grasses instead of forest. From opening day until August 1, when bait-fishing season ends and tighter trout limits go into effect, Crowley's the place to haul in big trout under a big, open sky, with big mountains lined up across the 395. From August 1 through October, people still fish (with restrictions), but they share the lake with sailors, jet-skiers and waterskiers.

Grant Lake

Grant Lake Marina
Hwy. 158 (June Lake Loop)
(760) 648-7964

Motorboats $40 for all day

The largest and least attractive of the June-area lakes, Grant is nonetheless a fun spot if you're a waterskier or jet-skier. You'll have to bring your own equipment, though—the little marina doesn't rent it. Early mornings are saved for fishing; boats can't go above ten miles per hour before 10 a.m. But after that, it's full-throttle fun.

Gull Lake

Gull Lake Marina
Off Hwy. 158 (June Lake Loop), June Lake
(760) 648-7539

2-person paddleboats $10 for 1 hr.
4-person paddleboats, canoes and rowboats $15 for 1 hr.
Kayaks $18 for 1 hr.
16-ft. motorboats $27 for 2 hrs., $37 half-day

I'm partial to this small lake next to June—it has tree-lined shores, a great view of Carson Peak, a good supply of large trout and a pretty, reasonably priced little marina. Also, its size and siting help protect it when the afternoon Sierra zephyrs blow. This little lake is particularly nice for families: There's a playground on its shores, a trout pond for feeding fish, friendly ducks who also want feeding, kid-pleasing paddleboats in the marina and picnic tables on the lakeview deck.

June Lake

June Lake Marina
Off Hwy. 158 (June Lake Loop), June Lake
(760) 648-7726

Motorboats $40 for half-day, $45 all day

Run by the same folks who run Crowley Lake Fish Camp, this is a small but professional marina on a beautiful glacier-formed Sierra lake, with the conveniences of the town of June Lake right at hand. Next to the marina is a small beach for sand play and swimming, although if you want to enjoy a proper lake swim—and this is the best lake in the entire region for swimming—head to the designated swim beaches across the lake (reached via the Oh! Ridge Campground). June is stocked regularly with various kinds of trout, and the marina store has a good supply of boats, tackle supplies, snacks and cold drinks. This marina rents only motorboats, but next door at Big Rock Resort you can rent a kayak or paddleboat.

Lake George
Woods Lodge Marina
Lake Mary Rd., Mammoth
(760) 935-4301

Rowboats $10 for 1 hr., $20 half-day
Motorboats $16 for 1 hr., $35 half-day

Lake George is one of my favorite Eastern Sierra lakes, blessed with beauty and accessibility. Crystal Crag looms overhead, pine trees line the shore, and small boats putter all summer long. More a hut than a marina, the tiny boat-rental place is run by Woods Lodge, which has cabins overlooking the lake (see page 55). If you need tackle, head for the general stores at Lake Mary or Twin Lakes.

Lake Mary
Lake Mary Marina & Store
Lake Mary Loop Rd., south end of Lake Mary, Mammoth
(760) 934-5353

Rowboats $15 for 1 hr., $25 4 hrs.
Paddleboats $15 for 1 hr.
Pontoon boats $50 for 1 hr., $135 half-day

The largest of the Mammoth Lakes, Lake Mary is a pretty one. Fishing is the main activity here, with trout that often reach trophy size. But some folks are happy just to row and putter. A tree-shaded campground and a cabin resort (Crystal Crag Lodge) are tucked among the trees along Lake Mary's shores, as is the small marina and good general store.

Mono Lake
See page 199.

Rock Creek Lake

Rock Creek Lake Resort
Rock Creek Rd., 9 miles up from Tom's Place
(760) 935-4311

Rowboats $18 for half-day, $28 all day
Motorboats $38 for half-day, $49 all day

The friendly people here can rent you a simple powerboat or rowboat on gorgeous Rock Creek Lake, where the fishing is good, the aspen trees ripple, and the water is cold (you're about 10,000 feet high). Dramatic peaks, some pocketed with snow even in August, soar overhead. Unlike so many rock-lined Sierra lakes, this one has many soft beaches. An easy hike up the Morgan Pass trail will take you to several other lakes, including Long Lake, all with good fishing.

South Lake

South Lake Boat Landing
2100 S. Lake Rd., off Hwy. 168, 30 minutes west of Bishop
(760) 873-4484

Motorboats $15 for 1 hr., $40 half-day, $55 all day
Pontoon boat $120 for half-day, $175 full day

A large, High Sierra reservoir at the head of Bishop Creek, South Lake is a first-rate fishing destination. Because it's more isolated than Crowley and the Mammoth lakes, and because lodging facilities are limited in the area, it is much less crowded than most area fishing lakes. And it is frequently stocked with brown trout and Alpers rainbows. This isn't a lake for swimming or water sports—it's all about fishing. (Plenty of hikers come here, too, because of the wonderful trailheads.)

Twin Lakes
Twin Lakes Store
Twin Lakes Rd. loop, off Lake Mary Rd., Mammoth
(760) 934-7295
Rowboats $8 for 1 hr.

The atmospheric old general store within Twin Lakes Campground will rent you a simple boat and sell you tackle for an outing on Twin Lakes, which is just across the road. If you don't fish, you can still go out for a row—head over to the waterfall for a particularly lovely outing. (Near the waterfall is also a prime spot to fly-fish.)

TENNIS

Mammoth Community Center
Minaret Rd., Mammoth
(760) 934-0150
www.ci.mammoth-lakes.ca.us/parkrec/index.asp

The city of Mammoth has a half-dozen good, free courts in the Community Center park available for drop-in play. Check first, however, in case there's a tournament or other event that's tying up court space.

Snowcreek Athletic Club
Old Mammoth Rd., Mammoth
(760) 934-8511
www.snowcreekresort.com/sac/index.html

This full-service athletic center includes a nine-court tennis complex, which is home to the Charlie Moore Tennis Academy throughout the summer. (Moore runs his program at the Desert Princess Country Club in Palm Desert the rest of the year.) Moore offers well-run, reasonably priced tennis clinics ($12 for Snowcreek members, $16 for nonmembers) and private lessons, and he puts on a couple of tournaments during the summer. If you rent a condo at Snowcreek, you become a temporary member of the club; otherwise, you have to pay a reasonable fee for a short-term membership.

Year-round fun

BODYWORKS: GYMS, YOGA & MASSAGE

The Body Shop Sports Training

3059 Chateau Rd., Mammoth
(760) 934-3700

Open Mon.–Fri. 6 a.m.–9 p.m., Sat.–Sun. 8 a.m.–8 p.m.
Day rates not yet established

At press time, this formerly modest gym had just reopened after a major re-model, which turned the place into an 8,000-square-foot full-service gym. I couldn't get there to check it out, but it has a climbing wall, well-equipped cardio facility, quite large yoga room, two weight-training areas, massage cen-ter, retail center, tanning room, salon, snack bar and brand-new fancy locker rooms. If you're a gym rat, make sure to check this place out.

Double Eagle Creekside Spa

Hwy. 158 (June Lake Loop), 2 miles past June Mountain
(760) 648-7134
www.doubleeagleresort.com

You haven't lived until you've had a seaweed wrap by the side of Reversed Creek—or so say many Mammoth and June locals, who've put a Double Eagle spa day on their permanent wish lists for birthdays and Mothers' Day. Part of a lovely cabin resort, this spa is the finest in the Eastern Sierra, with an ex-perienced staff and first-rate facilities. One favorite is the Forest Massage, in which you walk fifteen minutes through the woods to find a little cabin, where you'll have your massage ($90 for 50 minutes). You can have everything from a mini-facial ($50) to a hot-stone massage ($90), as well as such salon services as pedicures and hair coloring. There are several multi-treatment packages, ranging from $250 to $415.

The facility also includes a fine fitness center, comprising a large indoor pool, a circuit-training center, free weights, treadmills, elliptical trainers and such classes as yoga, tai chi and spinning. Resort guests use the facility for free; outsiders pay $25 a day.

Friends of Yoga
95 Berner St. (off Minaret near the Village), Mammoth
(760) 914-0105
www.friendsofyoga.com

Classes $7 each, 5 for $25

A group of massage therapists from In Touch opened this small yoga studio, which specializes in beginning and intermediate hatha and therapeutic yoga. The affordable, friendly, 90-minute classes are a great way to tune up for skiing, climbing or hiking.

In Touch Micro Spa
3325 Main St., Mammoth
(760) 934-2836

Hours vary; treatments by appt.

This well-established Aveda spa offers a number of appealing treatments, from the Hot Creek (a hand-and-foot thermal treatment) to the Mono Lake, a hot aromatherapy cocoon wrap. The ordinary massages and facials are first-rate. If you can snag a massage appointment with spa owner Carrie Meyers, who typically only works Sunday and Monday, you'll be a happy person. Prices range from $10 for a foot bath, to $70 for an "ultimate" one-hour massage, to $210 for the works.

Snowcreek Athletic Club
Old Mammoth Rd., Mammoth
(760) 934-8511
www.snowcreekresort.com/sac/index.html

Entrance free to renters or owners at Snowcreek; otherwise $17 for 1 day, $45 for 3 days and $170 for a 1-week family membership

The best gym in town is found at the only real athletic club in town, Snowcreek. It's a full-service fitness facility: nine tennis courts, five racquetball courts, basketball, volleyball, squash, indoor and outdoor pools, fitness classes (yoga, abs, step, swing dance, kickboxing), weight machines, free weights, spas, steam rooms, trainers and a good child-care facility. It's a shame the place wasn't designed to take better advantage of the magnificent Sierra views outside—from the inside, you could just as easily be in Montebello as Mammoth—but it's a quality athletic club with all the bells and whistles.

Stillpoint
452 Old Mammoth Rd., #D, Mammoth
(760) 934-7438
www.still-point.com

Appointments available daily 9 a.m.–9 p.m.

Offering a full roster of body-pampering services, from hot-rock massage to mineral salt scrubs, deep-tissue massage to gentlemen's facials, Stillpoint is a well-established and respected day spa. Treatments include an $85 salt scrub, a $75 one-hour massage, a $75 face-lift facial massage and the usual assortment of waxing, massages and facials. Its staff also does home visits, which cost more, of course.

ENTERTAINMENT

Booky Joint Video
437 Old Mammoth Rd., Mammoth
(760) 934-2176

Open daily 8 a.m.–10 p.m.

The Booky Joint's selection of rental videos and DVDs is pretty amazing, given how small the shop is. It carries all the new stuff, as well as an intelligent roster of older films. The magazine stand is full of interesting reads. Next door is the other half of the business, a fine bookstore.

Minaret Cinemas & Plaza Theater
Old Mammoth Rd., Mammoth
(760) 934-3131

The two-theater Minaret Cinemas and one-theater Plaza are under one ownership, and they're your basic small-town movie theaters. The Minaret is in the Minaret Village center on Old Mammoth Road, and the Plaza is just a block or so further up Old Mammoth. The theaters usually try to have one family-friendly movie in the mix, and there's always an action flick. Don't expect art films.

Wild Willy's Mammoth Arcade
Minaret Village Mall, Old Mammoth Rd., Mammoth
(760) 924-1082

Open daily in summer noon–9 p.m.; in winter, Mon.–Fri. 2–8 p.m.,
Sat.–Sun. noon–8 p.m.

A noisy, scruffy video-game arcade that will keep teens and other game junkies happy for awhile, Willy's also has computers with internet access.

FESTIVALS

Best of the Banff Mountain Film Festival
Late March
Bishop High School Auditorium, Bishop

Tickets available at Wilson's Eastside Sports, (760) 873-7520

This two-night festival always sells out well in advance, so get your tickets early. The films shown are the best representatives from the annual Banff Mountain Film Festival, an international competition showcasing films centered on adventure and mountain subjects.

Eastern Sierra Mountainfest
Late October
Tri-County Fairgrounds, Bishop
(888) 395-3952
www.mountainfest.org

These ain't no day-hikers—this two-day festival is for serious climbers, bouldering enthusiasts, backcountry explorers and adventure photographers. Talks are given by world-class mountain folk and photographers, the latest gear is on display, and bluegrass musicians play during the book signings and picnic lunch. Come only if you know the difference between a crampon and a piton.

Mammoth Lakes Jazz Jubilee

Mid-July
Various town locations
(760) 934-2478
www.mammothjazz.org

Founded in 1989 by a couple of local amateur musicians, the Mammoth Lakes Jazz Jubilee has grown to become the largest music festival in the Eastern Sierra. What started as a small concert by a local band is now a four-day festival featuring some 25 bands and attracting upwards of 20,000 people, including lots of retired folks. The focus is on traditional jazz, from Dixieland to swing to zydeco, but in recent years a little bit of modern stuff has crept in. Performances are held in about ten different venues, outdoors and indoors, in both the Old Mammoth and the Village areas; free shuttles connect the two festival areas. A jazz camp for teenage musicians coincides with the festival. It's a lot of fun, with town locals turning out in force to help, and lots of good music, dancing and conviviality.

Millpond Music Festival

September
Millpond County Park, north of Bishop
(760) 873-8014
http://inyo.org/millpond/

This small, sweet festival emphasizes world and folk music. Spread out your blanket, have a picnic and listen to a string band, an African ensemble or a first-rate fiddler. The most recent festival was a swell one, featuring Todd Snider, Laurie Lewis, Tom Russell, the Lovin' Spoonful and Fiddlin' Pete and Friends. Bring your instrument and join in one of the workshops.

Mule Days

Memorial Day weekend
Tri-County Fairgrounds, Bishop
(760) 872-4263
www.muledays.org

You say it's been a while since you've enjoyed a good session of coon jumping? Then mark Memorial Day weekend on your calendar for the annual Mule Days festival in Bishop. And coon jumping's not all—you'll also enjoy mule "pleasure driving," mule dressage, team roping, log skidding, barrel racing, mule chariot racing and all sorts of other rodeo-style fun starring the humble mule, along with a parade, a country-music headliner in concert, a big buffet dinner, a golf tournament, barbecue dinners and two country-western dances, one for families and one for adults. It's goofy as all get out, but full of old-fashioned rodeo fun. This hugely popular event has been going strong since 1969, drawing some 30,000 people, so plan early if you want to attend. It usually begins the Wednesday before Memorial Day weekend and ends on Sunday.

Sierra Summer Festival
Mid-July to mid-August
Various locations, Mammoth
(760) 934-2712, (888) 466-2666
www.sierrasummerfestival.org

After 27 years, this classical-music festival has matured into a well-rounded celebration of music both crowd-pleasing and challenging. Two weeks of the month-long festival are devoted to chamber-music performances held in St. Joseph's Catholic Church, featuring works from Mozart to Franck, with a children's concert for good measure. Then the Eastern Sierra Symphony Orchestra puts on a couple of blowout performances outdoors at Main Lodge; last summer's featured Tchaikovsky. Last summer also saw the festival conclude with what organizers hope will be an annual piano seminar, a week-long workshop bringing together students from North and South America with first-rate performing artists and teachers. This week also includes several performances for piano lovers.

HOT SPRINGS

I cannot claim to be the Eastern Sierra's expert on hot springs—that honor goes to George Williams III, whose book, **Hot Springs of the Eastern Sierra** (see page 229), will guide you to every worthwhile natural hot tub in the region. If you're a hot-springs buff, get this book. In the meantime, I can share my favorites with you.

First, a word about hot-springs etiquette. Do not be surprised if you see naked people at the more isolated springs. This is considered perfectly acceptable in the remote tubs. Stripping down at Keough's or Hot Creek, however, will get you kicked out (or worse) fast. Next, be respectful of others. Don't bring a boom box, don't be overly loud, and if the hot tub is crowded, wait until there's room for you—or, even better, until you have it all to yourself. Finally, please carry away all trash, and don't bring glass bottles.

Keough's Hot Springs
Off Hwy. 395, 7 miles south of Bishop
(760) 872-4670
www.keoughshotsprings.com

Open in summer Mon.–Thurs. 9 a.m.–8 p.m., Fri.–Sat. 9 a.m.–9 p.m.,
Sun. 9 a.m.–7 p.m.; in winter Wed.–Mon. 11 a.m.–7 p.m.
Admission $7 adults, $5 kids 12 & under

Unlike most other Eastern Sierra hot springs, Keough's is privately owned and developed, so you have to pay to use it. But if you have kids, it'll be worth it—they love this place. The centerpiece is a large swimming pool, complete with a couple of lane lines; it is fed with mineral water that's been cooled from its natural 122 degrees to a conventional heated-pool temperature. Kids especially love the huge waterfall-style mister on one end of the pool in summer (which gets hot in these parts). The numbers of people in the pool, especially in summer, mandate a small amount of chlorine, but not nearly as much as in a regular swimming pool (the mineral water is constantly being replenished from the spring). There's also a large, shallow soaking pool kept at about 104 degrees. Unlike at some hot springs, this water does not have that sulfur stink. There's a snack bar, a cheesy gift shop, changing rooms, showers and places to sit in the sun and the shade. Keough's is most definitely not a clothing-optional hot springs.

Hilltop Hot Tub
Off Benton Crossing Rd., 3.4 miles east of Hwy. 395, south of Mammoth
No phone

Some wonderful locals built a cozy concrete tub fed by pipes that bring in hot water from the spring that bubbles under the surface. Hilltop is one of a series of man-made tubs called the Whitmore Hot Tubs, all of which tap into water heated by the Long Valley Caldera; Hot Creek and Wild Willy's, below, are also considered Whitmore tubs.

Hilltop's location is spectacular, on a small rise in the middle of a huge prairie in the Long Valley Caldera, with snow-capped Sierras marching in a row to the west and the White Mountains lined up to the east. This is a small tub, so wait your turn if it's occupied when you get there. And know that this is often a clothing-optional place.

To find Hilltop, head east on Benton Crossing Road from Highway 395, where the green church is. When you pass the third cattle guard, you'll head down a hill. At the bottom of the hill, turn left on the dirt road and take it a few hundred yards to a dirt parking area. You'll see a small hill across a meadow in front of you—the tub sits atop that hill. You'll need a four-wheel-drive vehicle to get here in winter, and if there's been a big storm the road might be impassable, even with four-wheel drive.

Hot Creek

Hot Creek Hatchery Rd., off Hwy. 395, next to Mammoth Airport
(760) 924-5500 (Forest Service)
Open daily sunrise–sunset

Hugely popular with skiers, hikers, fishermen and pretty much everyone in the Eastern Sierra, this developed hot springs is maintained by the Forest Service. Follow the signposted dirt road past Hot Creek Fish Hatchery, just off the 395 next to the Mammoth Airport, and you'll come to a parking lot.(In winter this road may not be plowed, so access might be limited depending on your vehicle.) You'll see changing rooms off to the side and a trail overlooking the large hot pool in the gulch below. To reach the pool, you have to hike a short distance into the gulch. In winter, you might have to swim through cold water to get to the hot parts; in summer, all of Hot Creek is pretty warm.

Skinny dipping is not allowed—you need to find more remote hot springs for that—and neither are glass bottles. Please respect the site and do not bring in food and anything that might result in trash. And don't drink the water—it has traces of arsenic and other possibly toxic substances, including bacteria.

Finally, be warned that the water outside of the pool's boundaries can be fatal—thirteen people have died here. Hot Creek's source water is 200 degrees, which is the boiling point at this elevation. Being boiled is no way to perish. Do not let children wander, and do not take chances.

Wild Willy's

Off Benton Crossing Rd., 3.1 miles east of Hwy. 395, south of Mammoth
No phone

Not far from Hilltop Hot Tub, Wild Willy's has two man-made tubs, one a fairly large concrete one, the other a tiny wooden one. This is a good place for families, because it's safe—there's no risk of kids wandering off and getting burned like at Hot Creek. Take note that it is clothing-optional, and it's also popular, so you might be sharing with others.

To reach this spot, drive east on Benton Crossing Road from Highway 395. After the third cattle guard, make an immediate right on the dirt road. Staying left, drive that road for about a mile and park in the marked area. A trail (part of which is a wooden boardwalk over alkali that turns to muck when it gets wet) leads to the tubs. During snow season, you'll need a four-wheel-drive car to get here, and sometimes no vehicles can get through.

INTERNET ACCESS

If being away from your e-mail or your online communities is making you twitchy, here are a few places with computers and online access:

Access Business & Shipping Center
Minaret Village Mall, Old Mammoth Rd., Mammoth
(760) 934-4667
Open Mon.–Fri. 9 a.m.–6 p.m., Sat. 10 a.m.–5 p.m.
DSL and WiFi $3.50 per half-hour

Kava Coffeehouse
206 N. Main St., Bishop
(760) 872-1010
Open Mon.–Thurs. 7 a.m.–8 p.m., Fri.–Sat. 7 a.m.–9:30 p.m., Sun. 7 a.m.–4 p.m.
DSL-linked iMacs $3 for 1st 10 minutes, 10 cents per minute thereafter; WiFi free

The Looney Bean
Rite Aid Center, Old Mammoth Rd., Mammoth
(760) 934-1345
Open Sun.–Thurs. 5:45 a.m.–7 p.m., Fri.–Sat. 5:45 a.m.–9 p.m.
DSL $2 for 15 minutes, $7 per hour

Mammoth Lakes Library
960 Forest Trail Rd., Mammoth
(760) 934-4777
Open Mon.–Fri. 10 a.m.–7 p.m., Sat. 9 a.m.–5:30 p.m.
DSL free with 1-hour limit per day

Wild Willy's Mammoth Arcade
Minaret Village Mall, Old Mammoth Rd., Mammoth
(760) 924-1082
Open daily in summer noon–9 p.m.; in winter, Mon.–Fri. 2 p.m.–8 p.m., Sat.–Sun. noon–8 p.m.
DSL $7 per hour, $5 per half-hour

ONE COOL MUSEUM

Mammoth Ski Museum
100 College Pkwy. (off Meridian Blvd.), Mammoth
(760) 934-6592

Open Tues.–Sun. noon–5 p.m.
Admission $3 adults, $2 ages 5–18, college students free with I.D.; memberships available

Mammoth's development has its challenges and problems, but some fine things have come out of this prosperity: the improving hospital, the new community college and, now, the new Museum of Skiing. Dave and Roma McCoy, with particular help from Mammoth Lakes Foundation board member Warren Miller, were able to pull off a wonderful score: the collection of the late W. Mason Beekley, who passed away a few years ago. It is the finest collection of ski art in the world—and yes, there really is fine art depicting skiing.

The inaugural show wove together two themes: "The Art of Skiing" and "Skiing in History." Memorable works from that show included an Andrew Wyeth landscape, an extraordinary photograph by Leni Riefenstahl and a German ski poster with the most amazing intensity. And these two galleries of work, curator Finn MacDonald assured me, represented just a tiny fraction of the collection. The collection also includes a 2,500-volume library of ski-related literature going back to the 1500s, which is available to visiting scholars by request.

Curator Finn is usually on hand, and he's a wonderful and knowledge-able guide to the collection. Also worthwhile are the ski- and mountain-related films shown daily in the small theater. The gift shop showcases reproductions of artistically notable ski posters, along with books, frames and cool T-shirts. All in all, this is a fine little museum, an important addition to the ski community and a great refuge on a stormy day.

SHOPS WORTH KNOWING ABOUT

Booky Joint

437 Old Mammoth Rd., Mammoth
(760) 934-3240 (bookstore), (760) 934-2176 (video)

Bookstore open Sun.–Thurs. 8 a.m.–8 p.m., Fri.–Sat. 8 a.m.–9 p.m.; video store open
*   daily 8 a.m.–10 p.m.*

One side of this two-sided business is a fine small-town bookstore, with an excellent selection of topographic maps and regional guidebooks. You'll also find popular fiction, children's books, nonfiction best-sellers, art cards and music CDs. A hip selection of magazines is found next door in the video side (see listing under "Entertainment" above). The Booky Joint is also one of the unofficial town centers in Mammoth, where you can buy tickets for upcoming area events and where locals run into each other and catch up on gossip while looking for a good read.

Edisto Gallery & Tea Room

Sierra Center Mall, 452 Old Mammoth Rd., Mammoth
(760) 934-3001
www.edistogallery.com

Open Mon.-Sat. 10 a.m.-6 p.m.

Formerly funky Mammoth is getting more culturally sophisticated every year: Its independent bookstore is thriving, it has a new community college and ski/art museum, its summer classical musical festival is growing in stature, and now it has this lovely art gallery and tea room. Named for owner Mary Siceloff's home in South Carolina, Edisto has become a community center for local artists and art lovers, thanks to the regularly changing shows of local photographers, printmakers and painters. She also carries an irresistible line of fine-art crafts, from jewelry to ceramics; most are made by local craftspeople, but a few are "fair trade" items from Ten Thousand Villages, a nonprofit that helps artisans in Third World countries find markets for their work. The tea room serves 40 teas from around the world, as well as Looney Bean coffee and the wonderful baked goods from Bishop's Great Basin Bakery.

Footloose Sports

3043 Main St., Mammoth
(760) 934-2500
www.footloosesports.com

Open Mon.–Thurs. 8 a.m.–8 p.m., Fri.–Sat. 7 a.m.–9 p.m., Sun. 7 a.m.–8 p.m.;
*   summer hours may be shorter*

Footloose is owned by two of the friendliest guys in the Eastern Sierra, Tony Colasardo and master bootfitter Corty Lawrence (son of Olympic skier and local preservationist Andrea Mead Lawrence). People come from all over the state—even from other states—to buy skis, mountain bikes and, especially, ski boots. The bootfitters are superb, particularly skilled in fitting customers with the orthotics called Superfeet. The try-before-you-buy demo program is smart—if you're going to sink $500 or more into a pair of boots, you'd better make sure they're comfortable on the mountain first. Footloose is also a good place to rent skis, snowboards, boots and, in summer, quality bicycles and baby joggers.

Kittredge Sports

3218 Main St., Mammoth
(760) 934-7566
www.kittredge.net

Open Sun.–Fri. 7 a.m.–9 p.m., Sat. 7 a.m.–10 p.m.

This outdoor-sports-oriented sporting goods store has a large, comprehensive selection of clothing, goggles, skis, boots, gear, gizmos and accessories, with a particularly good selection for downhill skiers. We come here when we need things like socks, hats, Camelbaks, helmets and ice scrapers—it always has exactly what we need. For larger-ticket items, we wait for the seasonal sales, which are excellent. Also of note are the rentals—you can rent everything from fly rods and sleeping bags to snowshoes and Nordic skis. The ski-repair department is reliable.

Mammoth Luxury Outlets

3343–3399 Main St., Mammoth
(760) 934-9771

Hours vary; call for details

Nothing like the vast outlet malls in, say, Cabazon and Lancaster, this is really just a small strip center with a few moderately discounted shops, along with a restaurant (Perry's) and a massage business. The "name" out-lets are Coach, Bass, Polo and Van Heusen; the selection is pretty good and the prices are below retail, but not dramatically so. The Book Warehouse is a handy place if you need something to read—everything in there is remaindered or closed out, and you can find good deals, including hardback kids' books for $4. Mammoth Outfitters is an overcrowded jumble of sports clothing and accessories, but if you're a patient looker, you can find names like Columbia and North Face at discounts.

My favorite shop in this center is one that isn't discount at all: Learning Express Toys. Even my 14-year-old, who ought to be too old for toys, loves it. The emphasis is on lively, colorful, creative toys, games and baby clothes. The friendly staff does a fabulous and free job of personalizing and gift wrapping, and there's a gift registry for kids.

Mammoth Mountaineering Supply

3189 Main St., Mammoth
(760) 934-4191
www.mammothgear.com

Open daily 8 a.m.–8 p.m.

As much a community center as a retail store, climber Dave Talsky's store stocks everything you could conceivably need for climbing, tele skiing, Nordic skiing, snowshoeing and backpacking. His crew is exceptionally friendly and helpful, sales are good, and the store hosts occasional events, including the annual January "Telebration" at Chair 2 (Stump Alley), featuring free telemark clinics. This is also a great place to rent equipment for everything from tele skiing to backpacking. The web site often has good sale items—and free shipping.

Mammoth Sporting Goods

Sierra Center Mall, 501 Old Mammoth Rd., Mammoth
(760) 934-3239
www.mammothsportinggoods.com

Open Sun.–Thurs. 8 a.m.–8 p.m., Fri.–Sat. 8 a.m.–9 p.m.

This all-around sporting-goods store is the best place in town to rent bikes, with a good selection, the lowest prices and friendly service, as well as a good free map of bike routes around Mammoth. The store also has competitive prices on all the toys you need for mountain fun, from skis to sleds, hiking boots to Camelbaks.

Tonik

The Village at Mammoth
6201 Minaret Rd., Mammoth
(760) 924-7727

Open Sun.–Thurs. 10 a.m.–8 p.m., Fri.–Sat. 10 a.m.–9 p.m.

A great little shop run by a couple of longtime locals, Tonik has much more personality than the Village it sits in. It carries fashion for women, with a few clothing items for bold men. It's worth going in just to see the small but highly amusing selection of shoes and handbags. The clothes are fun and not necessarily pricey, and the inexpensive silver jewelry is well chosen.

Wave Rave

3203 Main St., Mammoth
(760) 934-2471

Open daily in summer 9 a.m.–9 p.m., in snowboard season
Sun.–Thurs. 7:30 a.m.–9 p.m., Fri.–Sat. 7:30 a.m.–10 p.m.

Owned by snowboard star Steve Klassen, Wave Rave is the top snowboard retailer in the Eastern Sierra, a must-visit for any boarder. The staff is knowledgeable, and the selection is great. Summertime brings lots of skateboarding gear, as well as a cool skate park with a five-foot mini ramp and a vertical ramp; the skate park is open daily in summer 9 a.m. to dusk.

TWELVE GREAT
HIKES

Since coming to this Pacific land of flowers I have walked
with Nature on the sheeted plains, along the broidered
foothills of the great Sierra Nevada, and up in the higher
piney, balsam-scented forests of the cool mountains.
— John Muir, *John of the Mountains*

Of the dozens and dozens of day hikes in Mammoth and the Eastern Sierra, here are one dozen personal favorites. They range from easy strolls suitable for 5-year-olds to more ambitious all-day treks, and each has an "oh, wow" end point. A USGS-based map is provided for each hike.

Hiker's **heaven**

From craggy granite peaks to cold mountain lakes, wildflower-dotted meadows to aspen-lined creeks, the places an Eastern Sierra hiker can explore are spectacular. Ask any longtime resident of the region: They never tire of hiking the countless trails here, from the short walks right around Mammoth to the treks deep into the John Muir Wilderness.

The routes I feature are all day hikes, some as short as one mile and suitable for small children and the less-than-fit, and others up to six miles and requiring a moderate effort (one, to Valentine Lake, has the option of going as far as eleven miles). None require any special gear, training or fitness, and each one leads to a special "wow" place: most often a lake, but sometimes a waterfall or a killer view. The majority are in the Mammoth area, with a few scattered from outside of Bishop to near Mono Lake.

Those seeking more ambitious hikes, including world-class backpacking routes, can seek guidance from more dedicated resources than this one. The Inyo National Forest website (www.fs.fed.us/r5/inyo) is a great place to start; its bookstore page lists every backcountry guidebook and map a backpacker could hope for. REI, A16, Wilson's, Mammoth Mountaineering, the Booky Joint and Sport Chalet also carry guidebooks and maps for serious hikers.

If you don't want to risk snow and ice, the best months for hiking are July and August. May and June can be wonderful at the lower elevations, depending on the lingering snowpack; September and October bring fall colors and generally empty trails.

No matter when you hike, remember that Sierra weather can be mercurial. Always have a daypack equipped with a sweater, rain poncho and water.

Here's how I categorize hikes by difficulty:

→ **Very easy:** Even the youngest children and the out-of-shape hike-phobic can handle it.

→ **Easy:** Uphill, but not too much so; fun for most kids and my 69-year-old mother, who's in good shape but hates steep uphills.

→ **Moderate:** You'll have some notable uphill to contend with, but if you're reasonably fit, you'll be fine. Quit yer whining.

→ **Strenuous:** Can you say "vertical feet"? You can have a piece of pie with ice cream after these hikes.

A Note About Mt. Whitney

Our own Mt. Everest, Mt. Whitney is the one American mountain everyone wants to climb. At 14,496 feet, it is the tallest mountain in the lower 48 states, attracting hikers and climbers from all over the world.

Reaching Whitney's peak is something that any fit, healthy person can do—but that doesn't mean you should run out and do it next weekend. Far too many people underestimate what it takes to successfully ascend Whitney, and most of them end up quitting before they get to the top. You need to train for a high-altitude, 22-mile hike like this, and you need to give yourself time to adapt to the altitude or you're likely to get too sick to make it to the top. So while technically Whitney can be climbed in one twelve-to-eighteen-hour day (if you start at 4 a.m.), you're much better off camping at least two nights: the first night at Whitney Portal (8,000 feet) and the second at either Outpost Camp (10,360 feet) or Trail Camp (12,000 feet). Some people even spend one night at Outpost and one at Trail Camp, to both better acclimate and to enjoy the Sierras.

Because crowds were overwhelming the trails, permits to climb Whitney between May 1 and November 1 are now available by lottery only; 100 day-hike and 60 overnight permits are granted for each day. (Permits for off-season ascents are easy to get, but you'll have serious snow, ice and weather to contend with, so you'd better know what you're doing—or have a good guide.) The lottery takes place every February for the following season; last season only 57 percent of the people who applied for overnight permits got one. For details on the permit process and on climbing Whitney, go to the Forest Service's web page, www.fs.fed.us/r5/inyo/recreation/mt_whitney.html, or call (760) 873-2400.

For further information on climbing Mt. Whitney, see two books in Chapter 13, "Essential Resources": **Climbing Mt. Whitney** (Spotted Dog Press, $8.95) and **Best Short Hikes in California's South Sierra** (The Mountaineers Books, $15.95).

THE **BEST HIKES** FOR:

- *Getting a workout:* Valentine Lake
- *High altitude with low effort:* Rock Creek to Long Lake
- *A family outing:* Minaret Falls
- *Catching a fish:* Convict Lake
- *Geographic diversity:* Parker Lake
- *People in a hurry:* Panorama Dome
- *Wondrous views:* Ruby Lake, Crystal Lake
- *Seeing wildflowers:* Emerald Lake & Sky Meadows
- *Backpacking:* South Lake to Long Lake (and beyond)

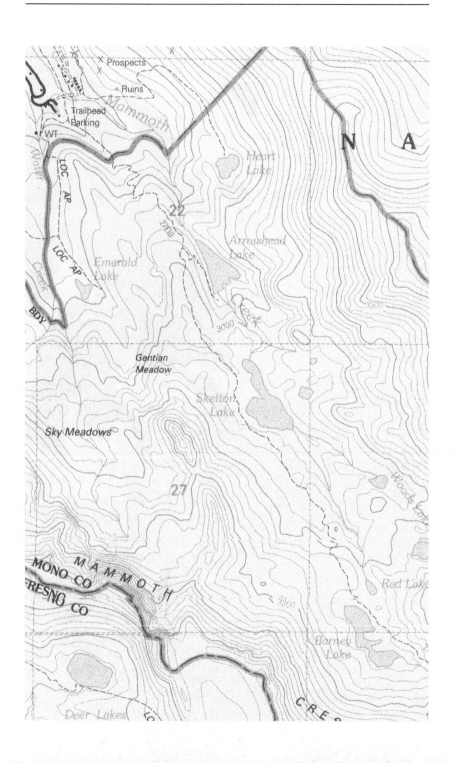

Arrowhead & Barney Lakes

Trailhead: Duck Pass trailhead, Mammoth
Directions: From Mammoth, take Lake Mary Road past Twin Lakes and turn left on
the road that goes around Lake Mary. At the end of the lake, take the dirt road
all the way through to Coldwater Campground to the trailhead lot.
Distance: 2.6 miles round-trip to Arrowhead, 5.4 miles round-trip to Barney
Difficulty: Moderate
Elevation at trailhead: 9,050 feet
Elevation at destination: 9,660 (Arrowhead), 10,200 (Barney)
Elevation gain: 610 feet to Arrowhead, 1,150 to Barney

You can hike as far as your legs will take you on the fine Duck Pass trail, which heads up Coldwater Canyon along Mammoth Creek to Arrowhead Lake, Skelton Lake, Barney Lake, Duck Pass and Duck Lake; from there it links to the John Muir trail, which will take you (or link you) to anywhere in the Sierras you care to go.

Most hikers, however, head for a lake. This is a busy trail, popular with short-haul fishermen and day hikers and long-haul backpackers and mule packers. In peak season you won't get a sense of isolation, but it's still a most rewarding trek.

The trail starts with a small switchback climb over a first hill. You'll then have an easier climb through pine forest; after almost a mile, Mammoth Creek will appear by your side. You'll reach a junction for the trail that leads down to blue, tree-lined Arrowhead Lake, which really is shaped just like an arrowhead; you can make this lake your destination, go down and see it, then head home. Or carry on a short distance to Skelton Lake, one side of which is sheer cliff. The next lake is Barney, my favorite destination. After leaving Skelton, you'll have a steep climb for a third of a mile, but then you'll be rewarded with a broad meadow thick with wildflowers. Then some more climbing and you'll come upon Barney, a shallow, rock-ringed lake that is the most amazing shade of emerald green (probably from algae).

If you're really ambitious, you can make the hearty climb over 10,797-foot Duck Pass and hike on to Duck Lake. It is dramatic in its contrast—because of its depth, it is an intense, dark blue, and because of its altitude, it has a barren, rocky setting.

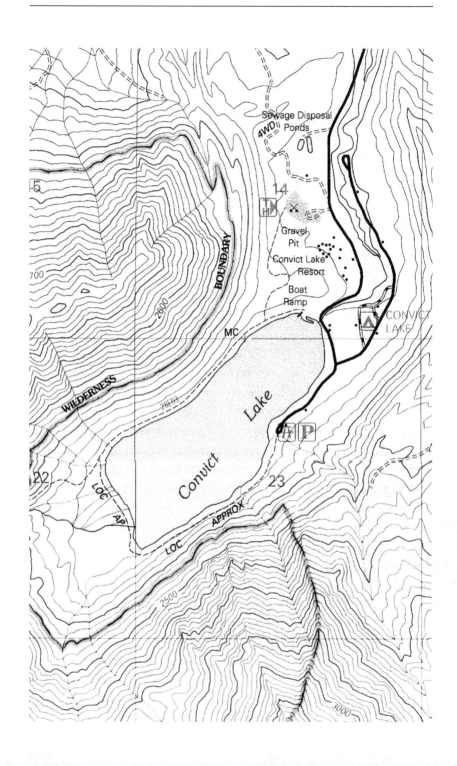

Convict Lake

Trailhead: At Convict Lake, 9 miles south of Mammoth
Directions: From Highway 395, take Convict Lake Road two miles to Convict Lake.
Pass the Convict Lake Resort and park at the lake. The trailhead is to the right of
the little marina and boat-rental shop.

Distance: 2.8 miles in a loop around the lake
Difficulty: Very easy
Elevation at trailhead: 7,640 feet
Elevation at destination: 7,640 feet
Elevation gain: Minor up and down on loop

It seems like most of the people hiking around Convict Lake have a fishing pole in one hand—the trail leads to countless fishing spots. But you hardly need to fish to enjoy this trail around deep, blue Convict Lake. Yes, there really were convicts here—in 1871 a posse chased an escaped gang into this canyon. The posse's leader, Robert Morrison, was killed in the ensuing battle, and the peak you see lording over the southwest side of the lake, Mount Morrison, was named for him. Nowadays, people entering this awesome spot are tracking trout, wildflowers and mountain views instead of bad guys, and they're usually successful.

This almost-three-mile trail loops gently around the lake. You'll start on the north side, on a sandy, dry trail, headed toward Mount Morrison and Laurel Mountain, with its gorgeous stripes of rust, gray, brown and white. When you reach the west end of the lake, you'll enter woods of aspen and cottonwood and cross over the many-branched Convict Creek via a long wooden walkway. On the south side of the lake, you'll head back toward the marina through sparse forest. You'll see plenty of places to stop and cast a fly—or enjoy the view—if the mood inspires you.

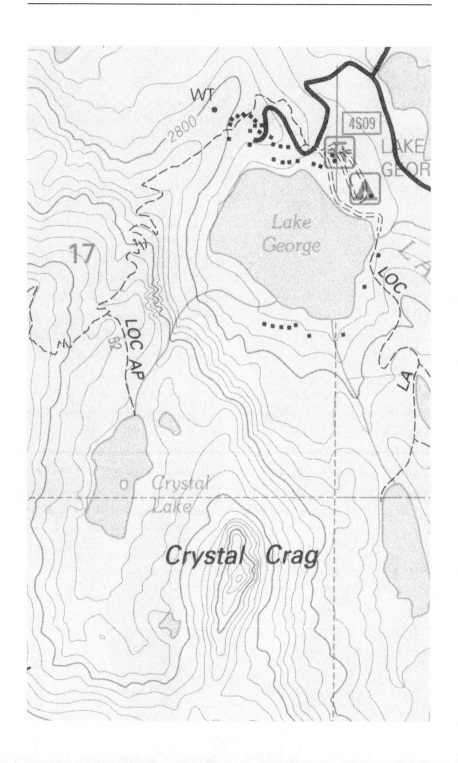

Crystal Lake

Trailhead: Lake George day-use parking lot, Mammoth
Directions: Take Lake Mary Road from Mammoth, past Twin Lakes. Follow signs to
Lake George and park in the day-use lot. The trailhead is the first one to the
right as you enter the parking lot.

Distance: 2.8 miles round-trip, more if you explore the lake
Difficulty: Moderate
Elevation at trailhead: 9,008 feet
Elevation at destination: 9,640 feet
Elevation gain: 632 feet

It's a workout, climbing up the ridge along the west end of Lake George, but I've seen 7-year-olds do it happily. Opinions vary on the distance from the trailhead to the lake: Some say 1.3 miles, some say 1.4, and one map says 1.75. I put the middle estimate, but when I hiked it, it sure seemed like 1.75 going up. But it was worth every step: After a climb through shady, pine-covered hillside above the Woods Lodge cabins, you walk along ridges with drop-jaw views of Lake George below and Lake Mary beyond. As you keep climbing, the views just get better, adding in the White Mountains off in the distance and Crystal Crag lording above. You'll reach a fork in the road, which is signposted; head left toward Crystal Lake, saving the other direction (Mammoth Crest) for a day when you want a really good workout. After a little more climbing you'll reach your highest hike elevation, then drop down to shimmering Crystal Lake, overseen by Crystal Crag.

This hike is well worth bringing a picnic lunch, especially if you're hiking with kids; wander the trail on the left side of the lake and you'll find plenty of picnic spots, as well as good spots for swimming (it's cold but tolerable, especially on a hot day), rock-skipping and perhaps even fishing.

Retrace your steps on the way down. The views are just as amazing on the return trip.

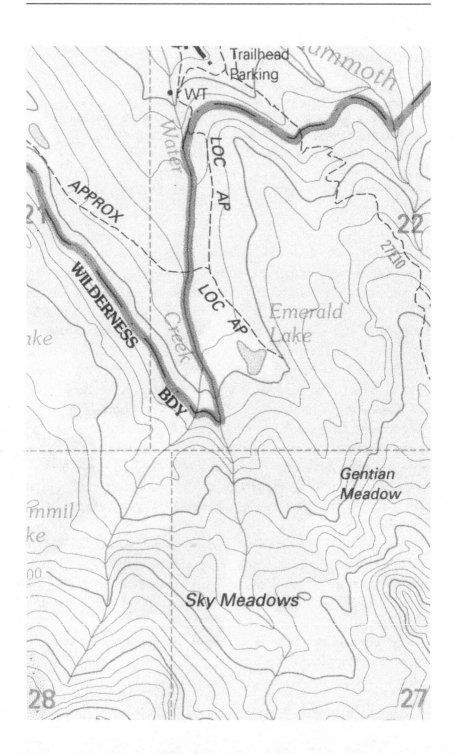

Emerald Lake & Sky Meadows

Trailhead: Signposted at the trailhead parking lot at the end of Coldwater Campground, Mammoth

Directions: From central Mammoth, take Lake Mary Road past Twin Lakes and turn left on the road that goes around Lake Mary. At the end of the lake, take the dirt road to Coldwater Campground and park in trailhead lot after passing through the campground.

Distance: 1.8 miles round-trip to Emerald Lake, 4 miles round-trip to Sky Meadows
Difficulty: Easy to Emerald, moderate to Sky
Elevation at trailhead: 9,050 feet
Elevation at destination: 9,440 feet (Emerald), 9,700 feet (Sky)
Elevation gain: 390 feet to Emerald, 650 feet to Sky

If you're a wildflower buff, this is the hike for you. At its peak glory in July and August, this trail leads to small, bright-green Emerald Lake, a short hike that's perfect for families. You'll climb through shady pine forest along Coldwater Creek, which provides water for a variety of mountain flowers. And the flowers get better when you reach the lake, especially by its inlet.

If a short hike is all you're up for, stay and enjoy Emerald Lake and head back the way you came. But you won't be sorry if you keep climbing up to Sky Meadows and its amazing wildflowers. When you reach Emerald Lake, head around the left side, looking for the inlet; climb up the trail along that inlet stream. You'll reach Gentian Meadow, where blue gentian runs riot in August. Cross Coldwater Creek and follow the trail uphill to a waterfall, then one more climb to reach small, protected Sky Meadow, which sits at the base of imposing Blue Crag. Snow can linger here into August, feeding wildflowers until late in the season. The flowers here are often tiny and alpine: paintbrush, blue and white gentian, California corn lily, elephant head, willows, white columbine, Sierra primrose and more. Take care not to trample the flowers, take some photos and, when you're ready, head back down the way you came.

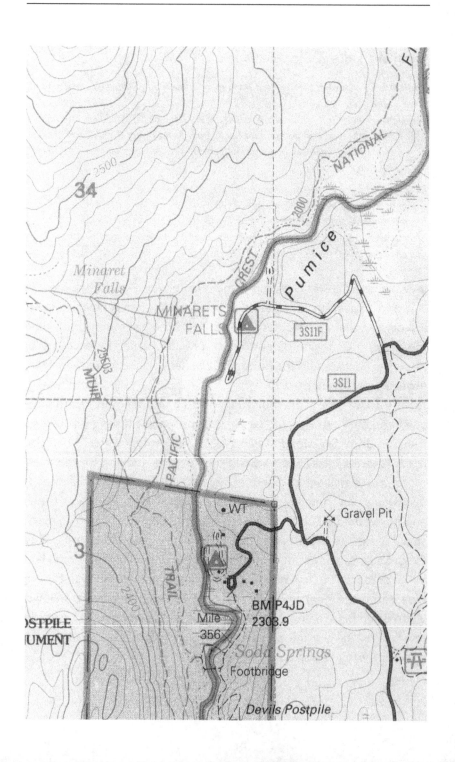

Minaret Falls

Trailhead: Along the short trail from the Devil's Postpile Ranger Station to Devil's Postpile, Mammoth

Directions: Take the mandatory shuttle to Devil's Postpile Ranger Station. Walk toward the Postpile, then cross a bridge, following signs to Minaret Falls.

Distance: 3 miles round-trip
Difficulty: Very easy
Elevation at trailhead: 7,559 feet
Elevation at destination: 7,650 feet
Elevation gain: 91 feet

In one relaxed, beautiful hike, you get to spend time on both the famed Pacific Crest Trail and the John Muir Trail—and you get to see Minaret Falls tumbling gradually over boulders into the San Joaquin River. For many people, this is a more rewarding, and much less populated, hike than the one down to Rainbow Falls.

Start at Devil's Postpile Ranger Station. Most people will first walk the short half-mile to see Devil's Postpile, a most amazing geological wonder. Then, if you're at all like me, you'll be itching to get away from the people (large women carrying tiny dogs, screaming toddlers, arguing spouses…). So follow the signs to Minaret Falls. You'll cross a beautifully built arched bridge over the San Joaquin River; just after you cross, look to your right to see if you can spot the soda springs, natural volcanic springs that bubble up here. In short order you'll be on the John Muir Trail, walking through forests of pine. You'll come to a crossroads and veer right on the Pacific Crest Trail (again, well marked toward Minaret Falls). When you hear the sounds of rushing water, look to your left, and you'll see the falls. You can head a little off trail here, going up to explore the falls; in late summer, when the water flow is less intense, they can be great fun for kids to play around, climbing the boulders and getting splashed.

From here most people turn around and head back. If it's late summer, and the water is low and calm on the San Joaquin, you can take off your shoes and ford the river over to Minaret Falls Campground, then walk one mile up the dirt road to catch the shuttle at the campground stop. Don't try it if the river has any oomph to it, though—you can end up washed downstream in a hurry.

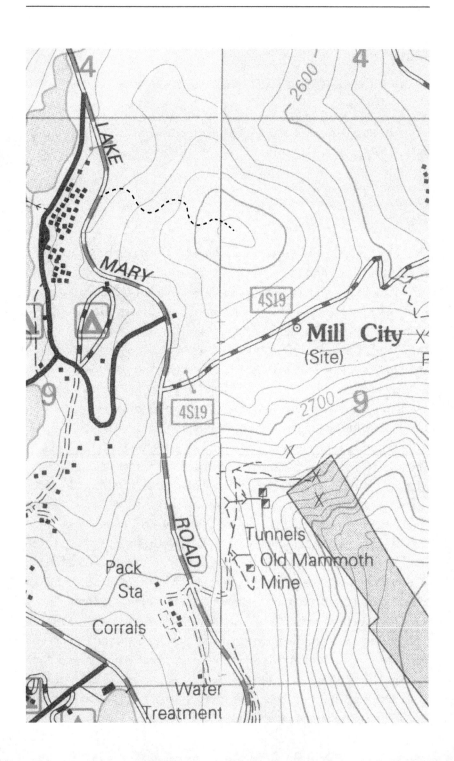

Panorama Dome

Trailhead: Signposted, along Lake Mary Road in Mammoth
Directions: Drive on Lake Mary Road between Twin Lakes and Lake Mary, and you'll
see the sign on the east side of the road. (You can park on the side of the road;
many walk here from their campground or cabin.)

Distance: 1 mile round-trip
Difficulty: Easy
Elevation at trailhead: 8,540 feet
Elevation at destination: 8,892 feet
Elevation gain: 352 feet

This is a fairly steep but quite short climb, just a half-mile up through imposing red firs; you might even pass a snowbank, even in hot summer months. The payoff is wonderful: In no time at all, you'll be on a windswept, sagebrush-covered dome, with views all around you: Crystal Crag, Mammoth Crest, Mammoth Mountain and more. You'd want to throw your arms out and run around the hilltop belting out "The Sound of Music," if it wasn't for all that sagebrush scratching your ankles.

After cruising around the top of the dome and taking in all the views, head downhill the way you came.

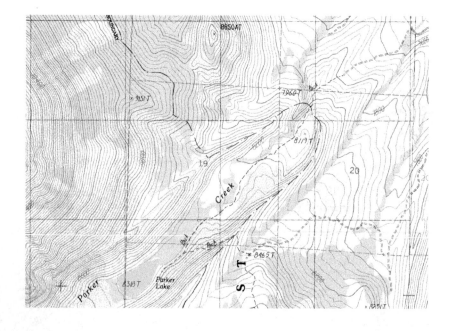

Parker Lake

Trailhead: At the end of the Parker Lake dirt road, between Mono Lake and June Lake
Directions: Enter the northern end of the June Lake Loop (Highway 158), south of Lee
Vining. A signposted dirt road to Parker Lake will appear in 1.5 miles. The 2.3-mile
dirt road ends at the trailhead. No facilities (restrooms, water) at the trailhead.

Distance: 3.8 miles round-trip
Difficulty: Easy/moderate
Elevation at trailhead: 7,950 feet
Elevation at destination: 8,400 feet
Elevation gain: 450 feet

This is the best hike in the region to experience the diversity of geology, flora and fauna in the Eastern Sierra. The first half-mile or so is the hard part, an uphill tramp through typical Eastern Sierra desert: a sand trail through sagebrush, bunch grass and other scrub, with lizards darting ahead of you. As you climb higher, you'll start to hear rushing water, and far down below to your right you'll see a line of Jeffrey pines indicating where Parker Creek flows.

The next mile and a half will be an easy stroll through gradually changing terrain. Ahead of you are towering, snow-pocked peaks; marking either side of the canyon are rocky moraines, left there by the glacier that powered through this canyon during the last Ice Age. You'll start seeing small aspens and some wildflowers; after a while Parker Creek will appear on your right. You've now entered the world that water brings: grasses and flowers, Jeffrey and lodgepole pine, aspens small and large (the white trunks of many large ones have been marred by too many initial-carving hikers). Then the forest gives way, and Parker Lake ripples before you. Straight ahead, some four thousand feet above, are Parker Peak and Koip Peak.

In one 45-minute hike, you've gone from the desert to a High Sierra lake overseen by granite peaks. And then on the way down, about the time you re-enter the desert area, you'll have amazing views of Pacific-blue Mono Lake and its volcanic islands straight ahead; to your left will be the Tioga Pass heading to Yosemite, and to your right, the range of Mono Craters. All this, and one nice afternoon's hike!

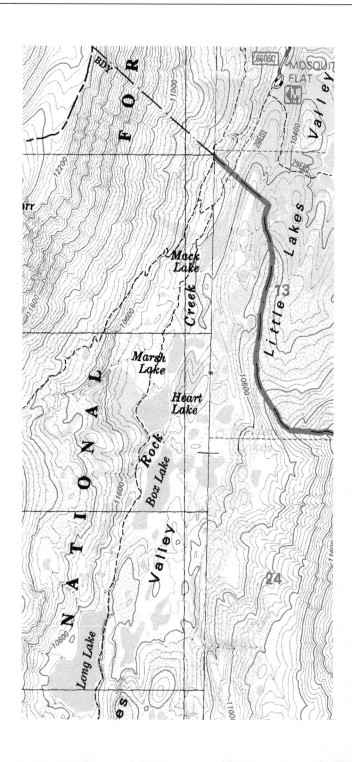

Rock Creek to Long Lake

Trailhead: Mosquito Flat, at the end of Rock Creek Rd., up from Tom's Place
Directions: From Highway 395, take Rock Creek Road up from Tom's Place. Take the
  road all the way until it ends, about 11 miles, past Rock Creek Lake. You'll see
  many cars parked.

Distance: 4 miles round-trip
Difficulty: Easy
Elevation at trailhead: 10,300 feet
Elevation at destination: 10,543 feet
Elevation gain: 243 feet

This family favorite wanders up Little Lakes Valley toward Morgan Pass, alongside Rock Creek and past meadows and wildflowers galore, to a series of beautiful High Sierra lakes, including Mack Lake, Box Lake and, finally, Long Lake. With Mount Mills, Mount Dade and Bear Creek Spire soaring 3,000 feet overhead (with snow clinging to them, even in August), the vistas are simply stunning. The fishing in these lakes is decent, and some brave souls jump in for a swim, but they usually jump right out—the water's cold up here at 10,500 feet! If you still have energy when you get to Long Lake, you can hike another .7 miles to Chickenfoot Lake, but be warned, it's a steep, strenuous .7 miles.

When you've had enough lake beauty, return to the trailhead the way you came.

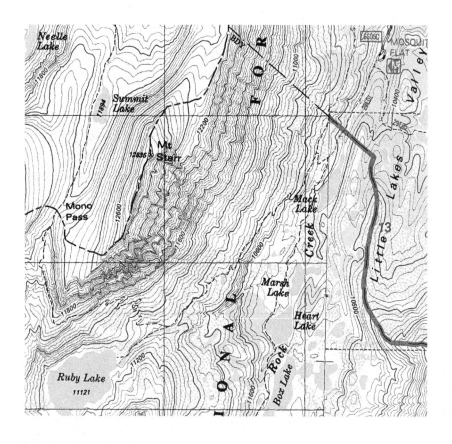

Rock Creek to **Ruby Lake**

Trailhead: Mosquito Flat, at the end of Rock Creek Rd., up from Tom's Place
Directions: From Highway 395, take Rock Creek Road up from Tom's Place. Take the
road until it ends, about 11 miles, past Rock Creek Lake. You'll see
many cars parked.

Distance: 4.2 miles round-trip
Difficulty: Moderate
Elevation at trailhead: 10,250 feet
Elevation at destination: 11,100 feet
Elevation gain: 850feet

A near-perfect High Sierra hike, this trail begins above 10,000 feet and takes you to about 11,000 feet, but not in a particularly taxing fashion (as long as you've acclimated to the altitude). The first leg is along the Morgan Pass trail, which also leads to Long Lake; it's a fairly steady but not too taxing uphill trek along a trail thick with wildflowers. Ahead of you is the wondrous Little Lakes Valley: Rock Creek running through meadows, leading to several small lakes, with fearsome peaks looming overhead. After a half-mile, you'll head right when the trail splits, following the sign to Mono Pass and heading up some not-too-grueling switchbacks. It's getting more forested now, and the views of Little Lakes Valley are getting better. A mile or so up, and then the trail levels out into a valley with a broad, green plain. Follow the sign toward Ruby Lake, walking along a creek, and soon the lake will open before you, with the Sierras towering behind it. Bring a picnic, a bathing suit if you're bold (it's brisk up here at 11,000 feet!) and perhaps a fishing pole (the fishing is reportedly fair.)

If you have an appetite for more, keep hiking up the trail to Mono Pass, a steep, two-mile climb that will take you above the 12,000-foot mark. You'll be rewarded with amazing top-of-the-world view.

Return the way you came, enjoying vistas as beautiful as on the uphill trek.

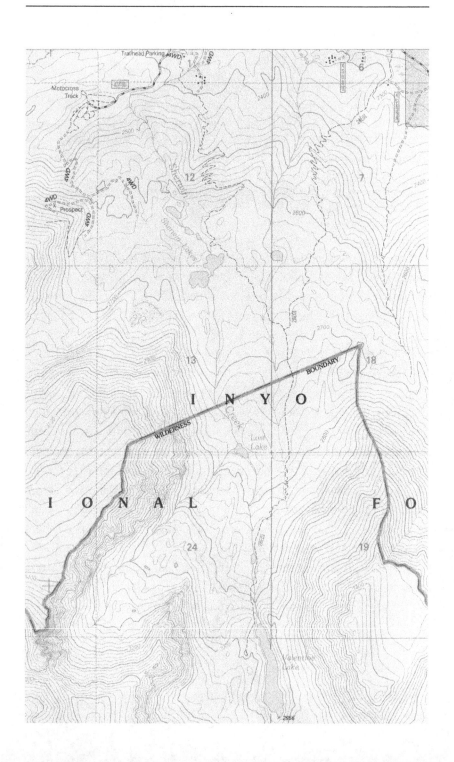

Sherwin & Valentine Lakes

Trailhead: Off Sherwin Creek Rd., Mammoth
Directions: From Old Mammoth Rd., take dirt Sherwin Creek Rd. (at the stables).
Drive 1.3 miles and turn right at the sign for the trailhead.

Distance: 4.5 miles round-trip to Sherwin Lakes, 11 miles round-trip to Valentine
Difficulty: Moderate/strenuous to Sherwin, strenuous to Valentine
Elevation at trailhead: 7,800 feet
Elevation at destination: 8,620 feet (Sherwin), 9,650 feet (Valentine)
Elevation gain: 820 feet to Sherwin, 1,850 feet to Valentine

Although the elevation gain is high on this hike, it's really not that tough, thanks to well-made switchbacks that minimize the uphill. You'll start by crossing over Sherwin Creek and heading up a dry, manzanita-covered hillside. The long, easy switchbacks will get you up the 800-foot, tree-studded granite moraine left by a glacier long ago. At the top, you'll have great views of Mammoth Mountain. You'll reach the Sherwin Lakes (there are five of them) and the trail to the first little lake. I prefer walking further on the main trail through the forest to the next trail junction, which heads off to the right and leads to the largest (and prettiest) of the lakes.

For most people, this is a plenty satisfying day hike. But if you have more in you, get back on the main trail and continue on about three more miles to Valentine Lake. You'll do some climbing, get some great views and head into the John Muir Wilderness. Once you're in the wilderness, you'll find yourself along an aspen-lined creek and discover wildflowers galore. But there's more hiking to do! You'll encounter Sherwin Creek again, and finally end your uphill hike at Valentine Lake, a heavenly spot with tree-lined shores and peaks overhead. Sit down and cool your feet in the cold lake—you've earned a rest.

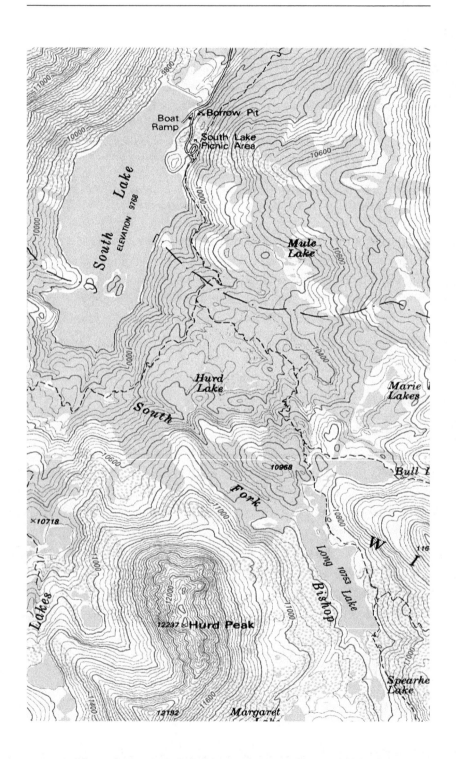

South Lake to Long Lake

Trailhead: Bishop Pass Trail, at the end of South Lake Rd., east of Bishop
Directions: From Bishop, head east into the mountains on Highway 168. After 15 miles,
   turn left on South Lake Road, taking the road all the way up to South Lake
   and the trailhead parking lot.

Distance: 4.6 miles round-trip
Difficulty: Moderate
Elevation at trailhead: 9,800 feet
Elevation at destination: 10,700 feet
Elevation gain: 900 feet

This superb hike takes you back into High Sierra wilderness. The trail continues on to Bishop Pass and links with other trails (including ones into Kings Canyon National Park), which is why you'll see backpackers setting out at the trailhead. But you can get a fine taste of this wilderness with a fairly easy 4.6-mile trek.

You'll start at large South Lake, a reservoir and popular fishing destination. The first part of the walk is an easy one, along the shores of South Lake, with peaks all around. You'll then climb through some trees. At the signposted junction for Treasure Lakes, stay on the trail to Bishop Pass. You'll gain elevation via some manageable switch-backs, and have some fine views. When you pass junctions for various destinations, stay on the main trail toward Bishop Pass.

Your destination will be deep, blue Long Lake, set in a lovely valley and surrounded by trees and boulders, with Mt. Goode rising above and the aptly named Inconsolable Range to your left, looking lonely and barren indeed.

Some hardy souls keep going several more miles to Bishop Pass, but I'm perfectly happy to stop at Long Lake, enjoying it for a spell before heading back down the trail.

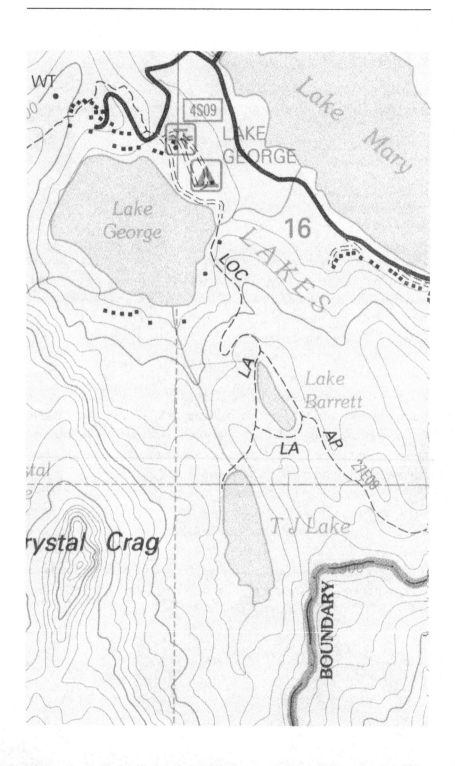

T.J. Lake

Trailhead: Lake George parking lot, near the campground, Mammoth
Directions: From the town of Mammoth, take Laky Mary Road and follow the signs to
*   Lake George. The trailhead is on the far end of the parking lot, clearly signposted.*

Distance: 1.8 miles in a loop
Difficulty: Easy/moderate
Elevation at trailhead: 9,008 feet
Elevation at destination: 9,260 feet
Elevation gain: 252 feet

Other guides label this hike "easy," but while it is short and the elevation gain is modest, there's one uphill stretch steep enough to make
kids whine and grandmas complain. But tough it out—it's worth it. At
the top of the climb through shaded forest you'll find Barrett Lake, not
particularly beautiful but worth a layover if you want to swim—its protected, shallow water is warmer than most local lakes, and less riddled
with fish hooks, so it's more fun for swimming.

An easy meander past Barrett Lake leads you to T.J., a more typically lovely High Sierra lake, rugged and shimmering, ringed with
pines and overseen by Crystal Crag.

After enjoying the lake, most people turn around and go back
the way they came, but I much prefer the trail that follows the stream
feeding out of T.J. To find it, take the main trail to the lake shore, then
turn right and follow the trail along the shore. You'll be at the stream
side very quickly; when in doubt, stay left along the stream, and head
downhill. It can get slippery in spots, so be careful. You'll enjoy cool
forests, splashing water and diverse greenery and wildflowers. You'll
end up on the shore of Lake George; turn right on the trail that heads
toward the parking lot. After you ford a little stream, and perhaps go
through a tunnel of greenery, you'll be back where you started.

GONE
FISHING

Trout fishing regarded as bait for catching men, for the saving of both body and soul, is important, and deserves all the expense and care bestowed on it.

— John Muir, *Our National Parks*

The Eastern Sierra is considered one of the best fishing areas in the country, so if you don't get out there and cast a fly or sink a line, you're missing out. This chapter will get you inspired, equipped, instructed and settled at just the right river, stream or lake to catch a fish.

The **fishing** basics

Astonishing numbers of fishermen visit the Eastern Sierra each year, most of them during the formal fishing season. And yet except for at opening-day festivities, early spring on Hot Creek and during a few derbies, you'd never know it—Inyo National Forest alone has 500 lakes and 1,100 streams, so there's room for everyone to spread out.

Here are some things you need to know to fish in Mammoth and the Eastern Sierra:

→ **Fishing season:** Fishing season for much of the region begins the last Saturday of April and goes until November 15th.

→ **Off-season fishing:** Some lakes and streams are approved for year-round fishing. These include Diaz Lake outside of Lone Pine and the Lower Owens River south of Pleasant Valley Dam (some areas are restricted to catch-and-release only). And some creeks open on March 1 for an early season; these include Independence Creek, Tuttle Creek, Cottonwood Creek and Lone Pine Creek.

→ **Licenses:** If you are over 16, you cannot fish in the region without a license. An annual license for California residents is $32.80; a two-day license is $16.55. Each season there are two exceptions to this: The second Saturday in June and the last Saturday in September are free fishing days. Licenses are available at fishing retailers and general stores all over the Eastern Sierra. You'll get a stiff fine if you are caught fishing without a license, so don't try it. Besides, license fees are an important source of funding for the state's fish-hatchery program, without which you'd have no fish to catch.

→ **Limits:** Other than in catch-and-release locations, limits are usually five fish per day, and you can't have more than ten fish in your possession at any time. At Crowley Lake, that limit drops to two fish per day from August 1 until the end of the season. At Hilton Creek downstream from Crowley, the Upper Owens River just upstream from Crowley and McGee Creek east of Highway 395, the weeks before Memorial Day and after October 1 have a barbless-hook rule and two-fish limit.

→ **Restrictions:** Watch for posted restrictions. Some spots, such as McCloud Lake and Hot Creek, allow catch-and-release fishing only and forbid barbed hooks. Respect these rules: The future of the trout population depends on it.

→ **The DFG:** Without California's Department of Fish and Game (DFG), which propagates and plants millions of trout and regulates the sport, there'd probably be no fishing in the Eastern Sierra—it'd have been fished out decades ago. Its web site, www.dfg.ca.gov/fishing, is a great place for information on hatcheries, regulations, recent fish plantings, fishing-related festivals and more. The site also has an amazing topographical-map-based guide to fishing in California. And if you see some-one polluting your favorite stream or fishing out of season in a restricted area, call its Cal-Tip line, (888) 334-2258.

Best **fishing shops** & instruction

Brock's Flyfishing
100 N. Main St., Bishop
(760) 872-3581, (888) 619-3581

Open Mon.–Sat. 7 a.m.–6 p.m., Sun. 9 a.m.–5 p.m.
www.brocksflyfish.com

A long-established, full-service fly-fishing shop, Brock's is also known for its guide services, seminars and classes. In the $150 four-hour Introduction to Flyfishing class, you'll learn everything from knot tying to streamside etiquette; or you can go straight to the more intensive two-day beginning fly-fishing seminar, which includes a day of fishing on the wild trout section of the Lower Owens and a barbecue dinner at the home of Brock's owners, Gary and Pat Gunsolley. When you're ready you can move on to the more advanced two-day nymphing (casting your fly so it's just under the water's surface) seminar, held on the Lower Owens River or Hot Creek.

Brock's sells a full range of fishing supplies, including locally tied flies, and rents everything from wading boots to pontoons to fly rods. It can also get you to the more inaccessible reaches of the Lower Owens River via drift boat. And its web site has up-to-date local fishing reports.

The Troutfitter

Shell Mart, Old Mammoth Rd. & Main St., Mammoth
(760) 924-3676, (800) 637-6912
www.thetroutfitter.com

Open late April–mid.-Nov. daily 6 a.m.–8 p.m., off-season daily 8 a.m.–noon;
off-season hours may vary

This is the sort of tidy, well-stocked fly-fishing shop where men stare lovingly at rods and flies, then talk about trout and fly-tying for ages with the friendly staff and other devotees hanging around. It carries a great range of Umpqua flies and lots of locally tied flies, as well as all the fishing accessories, from instructional videos to rod cases. Now owned by the larger Trout Fly next door, it shares the same guides as its parent; see "Guides & Fly-fishing Ranches," page 184.

The Trout Fly

Shell Mart, Old Mammoth Rd. & Main St., Mammoth
(760) 934-2517
www.thetroutfly.com

Open late April–mid-Nov. daily 6 a.m.–8 p.m., off-season daily 8 a.m.–noon;
off-season hours may vary

It seemed odd when the Trout Fly moved in right next door to Mammoth's other longtime fly-fishing haven, the Troutfitter, and the two seemed to go head-to-head. But in fact the larger Trout Fly bought the Troutfitter, and the two are pretty much the same business—they're just keeping their own names, much like modern marriages. Combined, the two have 4,000 square feet of retail space and, say the owners, nearly 250,000 flies. You'll also find complete fly-tying supplies, clothing, gear, accessories and rental and demo equipment. The Trout Fly's guides, some of whom are co-owners of the store, are among the best in the west; see "Guides & Fly-fishing Ranches," page 184.

Fish **hatcheries**

Alpers Owens River Ranch
See "Guides & Fly-fishing Ranches," page 182

Tim Alpers grew up on this ranch, which was run as a fishing lodge by his parents and remains one today. Now, in addition to being a private fly-fishing ranch, it is famous as a trout hatchery. Found only in the Eastern Sierra, Alpers trout are big ones, usually at least two or three pounds and sometimes as much as ten pounds. Tim raises some 60,000 pounds of trout a year here, most of which are planted in lakes and streams throughout the Eastern Sierra; a few of the pink-fleshed, delicious fish land up in the area's best restaurants (Convict Lake is a great place to sample Alpers trout). Unfortunately, you can't view this operation unless you're staying at the fishing lodge. But it's worth knowing about, because you'll see the term "Alpers trout" used constantly throughout the Eastern Sierra.

Hot Creek Hatchery
Hot Creek Rd., 2 miles south of Mammoth Airport
(760) 934-2664

Open daily 8 a.m.–4 p.m.

The DFG raises an astonishing three million trout a year here, as well as twenty million eggs for other hatcheries to use. Those three million fish are then planted in lakes and streams all over the Eastern Sierra. Because of its consistently warm water, which comes from a natural hot springs, this is an ideal spot to grow healthy, hearty trout. It's a lot of fun to take the brief detour off Highway 395 to see the operation, especially the raceways (long rearing ponds) stuffed full of fat rainbow trout.

Mt. Whitney Fish Hatchery
Off Hwy. 395, 2 miles north of Independence
(562) 590-5020 (DFG fish-stocking information)

Open Mon.–Fri. 7:30 a.m.–5 p.m., Sat.–Sun. 8 a.m.–5 p.m.
See listing in "Best Reasons to Stop" in Chapter 11, page 216.

Fishing **with kids**

"The best place to take kids fishing," says my fly-fishing friend Steve Terui, father of two, "is anywhere they plant trout." On Thursdays during fishing season, the DFG truck usually dumps nets full of trout into the Mammoth-area lakes and streams. Just follow the truck, watch while the DFG folks dump the trout in, then tell your kid to throw in a line. Guaranteed fish! Mammoth Creek, the various Mammoth lakes, Convict Lake, Convict Creek, Rock Creek and Rock Creek Lake are all good spots for family fishing, especially right after a new batch of trout has arrived.

If you're willing to spend on a private instructor and guide, try Sierra Drifters (see page 184). They're great with kids.

A big hit with kids is the annual Children's Fishing Festival, held in late July. The ponds next to Snowcreek's rental office on Old Mammoth Road are stocked with fat Alpers trout, and kids under 15 can catch away, with prizes awarded in all sorts of categories. Sponsored by local businesses, this fishing derby is free and a wonderful family outing; call (760) 924-2360 for information.

Guides & fly-fishing ranches

Alpers Owens River Ranch
Owens River Rd., east of Hwy. 395, 15 miles north of Mammoth
(760) 648-7334

Open April–Nov. 1; cabins $125 for 2 people, $45 for each additional adult & $20 for each additional child ages 5-12

It's damn near impossible to get a cabin at this fly-fisher's nirvana. Although he is perhaps the friendliest fish lover in the Eastern Sierra, Tim Alpers doesn't do anything to promote his ranch: no web site, no advertising, no publicity. That would just attract more people he'd have to turn away.

Tim's parents made this ranch into a fishing retreat, and he has earned fishing-world fame of his own by becoming California's preeminent trout breeder, supplying the Sierra's streams, lakes and restaurants with the huge Alpers rainbows. Nowadays he also runs the ranch, which still has the same nine basic housekeeping cabins, varying in size to accommodate between two and nine people. They're perfectly fine, but no one comes here for the cabins—they come here to fish. Located at the headwaters of the Owens River, Alpers is blessed with a private stretch that offers some of the finest fishing in the west (barbless catch-and-release, of course). The property also includes a one-and-a-half-mile tributary channel generously stocked with nice-size trout, where bait fishing is allowed and you can keep (and eat—they're superb) up to two fish a day; this stream is a big hit with kids.

Alpers says that 90 percent of his ranch guests return each year, which is why it's so hard to get a cabin. Previous guests get first dibs on the next season; if they haven't committed by January 1, space is opened for new-comers. So if you hope to stay here, get on the phone on January 1.

Fortunately, ordinary people can now fish at least part of the ranch. Tim maintains a five-acre lake stocked with trophy-size trout, and it's open to the public for three three-hour sessions daily. Fishing on this lake is via float tube only (bring your own—you can rent one in Mammoth or Bishop), and it's barbless and catch-and-release only. A three-hour session costs $45 ($40 if you're staying at the ranch).

Eastside Guide Service

Mammoth
(760) 924-8177
www.e-wave.com/esgs

Eastside is really Kevin Peterson, a co-owner of the Trout Fly and one of the best fishing guides in the west. He knows every place where trout can be found in the Eastern Sierra, he knows how to catch 'em, and he'll make the experience fun.

Hot Creek Ranch

Hot Creek Hatchery Rd., off Hwy. 395, 2 miles south of Mammoth Airport
(888) 695-0774
http://hotcreekranch.com

Open late April–Nov. 15; cabins for 2 $182 weeknights, $545 for 3-night weekend (minimum), $1,070 week; extra person $80 per night; children under 16 free

Rather like the serious sushi bars that expect patrons to eat exactly what the chef demands, Hot Creek Ranch has its standards. Dry-fly, catch-and-release fly-fishing only. No wading. Barbless flies only. No more than three fishing guests per cabin. No dogs. Three-night minimum on weekends.

If you follow these rules, and pony up the money for one of the nine cabins (each with two double beds and a kitchen area), you will be rewarded with access to a 2.5-mile private stretch of Hot Creek that is considered one of the best trout streams in California, kept at a constant 55- to 60-degree temperature by the nearby thermal springs. It's also a gorgeous spot, surrounded by multicolored grasses, with big skies overhead and mountains all around. For $75, you can take the 90-minute Introduction to Hot Creek Ranch Fishing class, which will set you up for days of good fly-fishing. They'll also book you one of the excellent guides found through The Trout Fly in Mammoth. And there's a good store selling supplies and flies that work well in these waters.

Some fly-fishermen find Hot Creek Ranch to have a little too much attitude; they prefer to explore the Owens River on their own or with an independent guide. But others swear by it and come back year after year.

Sierra Drifters
Mammoth & Crowley area
(760) 935-4250
www.sierradrifters.com

The general consensus among my serious fishing friends is that the very best guide in the region is Tom Loe, founder of Sierra Drifters. Great with experts and beginners, kids and adults, Loe is a Coast Guard–licensed captain and former commercial fisherman who can take you via drift boat to stretches of the Lower Owens River that you could otherwise never get to. Loe, and his staff of highly qualified guides, can also take you to the gorge above Pleasant Valley Reservoir, as well as to McGee Creek, Crowley Lake (via "fish magnet" flat boats), East Walker River and many other prime trout-fishing spots. They'll even guide you on a photography outing, if fishing's not your thing. Loe and his guides do a particularly good job with families, teaching kids to fish and setting up such adventures as float tubing on a beautiful Sierra lake.

The Trout Fly & The Troutfitter
Shell Mart, Old Mammoth Rd. & Main St., Mammoth
(760) 934-2517
www.thetroutfly.com

These two businesses have joined forces, so now they have an even larger roster of guides, including several women, and all are experienced and easygoing. Perhaps the best of the bunch is Kevin Peterson, a Trout Fly co-owner who also works in the shop. An outgoing, genial guy, he's been in Mammoth since 1981 and guiding in local waters since '88. But if Peterson's not available, you'll find someone good. Check out the web site, which has bios of many of the guides.

Lakes

→ **Convict Lake.** A trail encircles this spectacular, crystal-clear lake, making it a great place for shore fishing—there are plenty of spots. You can also rent a boat at the little marina, but head out early, because the wind can blow later in the day. The lake is typically rich in browns and rainbows. It is found via Convict Lake Road off the 395, a few miles south of Mammoth; go to www.convictlake.com for more information.

→ **Crowley Lake.** The granddaddy of fishing lakes in the Eastern Sierra, Crowley sits on a flat, grassy plain in the Long Valley Caldera south of Mammoth. It's hugely popular with all sorts of fishermen, from dry-fliers to bait-and-hookers, and it's the site of several fishing competitions, starting with the festivities on the first day of fishing season. Crowley's large marina rents boats and sells supplies, and plenty of guides work these waters. For information go to www.crowleylakefishcamp.com.

→ **June Lake & Gull Lake.** These next-door-neighbor lakes are stocked with Alpers trout, and the fishing is consistently good on both lakes. June is larger, with more room to spread out; Gull is more protected on windier days. Both are found on Highway 158, the June Lake Loop, off the 395 north of Mammoth.

→ **Lake Mary, Lake George & Lake Mamie.** Planted regularly with DFG rainbows, brooks and browns, these Mammoth lakes also receive honkin' big Alpers trout (ten to twelve pounders) from time to time. Lake Mary is the most popular fishing lake and the best one for fly-fishers to work, but George and Mamie are also fun for conventional bait- or lure-fishers. All three are popular with families, and all have little marinas with boat rentals and tackle. They are found off Lake Mary Road a few miles out-side of Mammoth.

→ **McCloud Lake.** Reached via an easy half-mile hike, this is a fine, uncrowded spot to fly-fish. The DFG stocks it regularly; fishing is restrict-ed to barbless hooks and catch-and-release only. The trailhead is found at Horseshoe Lake, at the end of the road that leads past Lake Mamie.

→ **Rock Creek Lake.** Besides beautiful Rock Creek Lake, another eleven lakes are scattered around this area, some a short walk from Rock Creek Lake, others an enjoyable hour's hike away. All of them are stocked, all are High Sierra gems, and none are crowded. Rock Creek Lake is found nine miles up Rock Creek Road from Tom's Place, just off the 395 between Bishop and Mammoth.

→ **Sotcher Lake.** Located near Devil's Postpile in the San Joaquin River valley, Sotcher is a pretty lake with wildflower meadows around it and hearty fish inside it. It's a swell place to fly-fish for rainbows, browns and Alpers biggies. To get here in summer you have to take the Devil's Postpile shuttle (www.nps.gov/depo has shuttle information) from Mammoth's Main Lodge, unless you're camping in one of the valley's campgrounds.

→ **Twin Lakes.** Rainbow trout swim in these waters, and people catch plenty of 'em—sometimes big ones. Fly-fishers go on the water early, and have particularly good luck over by the waterfall, but most of the day this is a bait-fishing lake. It is found on the Twin Lakes loop road off Lake Mary Road, just outside of Mammoth.

Rivers
& streams

If you put on your hiking shoes and head into the mountains, you'll find plenty more streams, but here are the best ones you can reach by car, with perhaps a short hike.

→ **Bishop Creek.** Stocked with both DFG and Alpers fish, this beautiful, rushing creek feeding out of South Lake is a great place to fish during the spring and first half of the summer. Sometimes in late summer the water gets low and the fishing more challenging—but if that's the case, just continue on up the road and cast a line on large South Lake, a mecca for fishermen. Bishop Creek parallels South Lake Road, reached off Highway 168 from Bishop.

→ **Hot Creek.** Considered one of the best dry-fly trout streams in the country, Hot Creek is warmed by a hot springs, which keeps the temperature consistently trout-friendly. The down side is that the stretch available for public fishing is short, so it can get far too crowded. But if you can find your spot, the catch-and-release fishing will be good, and the setting is lovely. This area is reached via Hot Creek Road east of Highway 395, just south of Mammoth Airport.

→ **Owens River.** The Upper Owens is the stretch running for fifteen miles north of Crowley Lake, including the Benton Crossing area. This is a gentle, shallow, sometimes marshy river winding through the Long Valley meadows. To reach the northernmost accessible section, head fifteen miles north of Mammoth on Highway 395 and go east on Owens River Road; in a couple of miles, you'll come across Big Springs campground, and the one-mile stretch of the Owens that starts here (at the headwaters) is open for public fishing in season. The next several miles belong to private ranches, including Alpers Owens River Ranch. Drive south past these ranches and you'll find a dirt road that will take you to the accessible parts of the Upper Owens, which can be fished in season all the way south to Crowley Lake. You can also get access to the Upper Owens from the southern route, by heading east on Benton Crossing Road off the 395, between Mammoth and Crowley Lake. The creek-like Lower Owens is found south of Pleasant Valley Reservoir, near Bishop; catch-and-release fishermen can ply these waters year-round. Although they aren't large, the brown trout are plentiful in the Lower Owens, and fishing here on a quiet winter day can be gorgeous, as long as you're dressed very warmly. Late-summer fishing can be less successful, if water levels are low. These lower stretches of the Owens are easy to reach off Highway 395.

→ **Mammoth Creek.** Running right through the town of Mammoth, from Twin Lakes to Hot Creek, this creek is stocked weekly by the DFG. It's a fun, easy place to fish, popular with families, who typically use salmon eggs for bait.

→ **Robinson Creek.** A fine and lovely creek that feeds Mono County's Twin Lakes, near Bridgeport. There are pleasantly funky cabin resorts and nice campgrounds around here. The section between Upper and Lower Twin Lakes closes to fishing on September 14th; the upper section allows catch-and-release only during the last month of the season. Reached via Highway 395, north of Mono Lake.

→   **Rock Creek.** A beautiful stream fed by a series of High Sierra lakes, Rock Creek is a fun place to fish, especially for fly-fishers. Rainbows are plentiful, and the creek (as well as Rock Creek Lake) is also stocked with big Alpers trout from time to time. It's found along Rock Creek Road up from Tom's Place, between Bishop and Mammoth.

→   **San Joaquin River.** This particularly beautiful river (actually the San Joaquin's middle fork) can be reached via Minaret Road, past Mammoth's Main Lodge; in summer you'll have to take the shuttle to get there (www.nps.gov/depo has shuttle information). You can catch golden, brook, brown and rainbow trout all from this one river, which is quite extraordinary—although last summer the river wasn't stocked because of DFG budget cuts, so the fishing wasn't up to its usual par. Hopefully that will change in the future. Set out from Minaret Falls Campground, Devil's Postpile or Red's Meadow to find a good spot.

TOP TEN SIGHTS
IN THE EASTERN SIERRA

*We all occasionally need to see a wild and sweeping
horizon just to keep from going crazy, and perhaps
nowhere else so close to a city are there more spectacular
panoramas than in the Eastern Sierra.*
— Gordon Wiltsie, *California's Eastern Sierra*

There's more to the Eastern Sierra than outdoor sports. Although
you might not know it if you just drive back and forth to the mountains
and lakes, there are fascinating sights a'plenty, from the eerily preserved ghost town of Bodie, to the wonder of salty Mono Lake, to the
reminder of the sad chapter of American history known as Manzanar.

Alabama Hills

Alabama Hills Recreational Area
Off Whitney Portal Rd., west of Hwy. 395, Lone Pine
No phone

I hesitated bringing my kids here, because these hills are famous for being the location of many a classic Hollywood Western—and few kids today have the slightest interest in old black-and-white movies. But I was wrong to hesitate. Whether or not you saw *Wagon Train* or *Gunga Din,* the Alabama Hills are really cool. For most over-50 folks, it's fun to drive or stroll through these amazing rock formations, remembering your favorite shoot-'em-up scenes. For kids and the young at heart, these thousands of smooth, rounded, almost lifelike-looking rocks are just begging to be scrambled on. Try to visit outside of July and August, when the heat can be oppressive for those venturing out of their cars; if temperatures are moderate, take time to walk, explore and scramble a little.

While you're exploring, look westward to the peaks of the Sierras, and marvel at how the Alabama's rounded boulder stacks are exactly the same age as the jagged granite peaks a few miles away. It was once assumed that the Alabama Hills were much more ancient than the fierce Sierras. But their vastly different appearance turns out to be due to different weathering. In the high altitudes, the granite peaks have been subjected to untold thou-sands of cycles of freezing and thawing, with the expanding and melting of annual snowfall. This led the peaks to crack and become more jagged and gray. Meanwhile, down in the Alabamas, a damp climate and soil-covered granite led to the soft-er-looking, brown-and-yellow rock we see today.

Ancient Bristlecone Pine Forest

Ancient Bristlecone Pine Forest Visitor Center
Schulman Grove
White Mountain Rd., 10 miles north of Hwy. 168 East, near Big Pine
(760) 873-2500

Open May–Oct., depending on snow conditions; call for hours

On the western flank of the stark, climatically hostile White Mountains, across the Owens Valley from the Sierras, lies this strange, sparse forest dot-ted with western bristlecone pines. Gnarled and stunted-looking, these hardy, slow-growing trees are well suited to survive the White's scarcity of water and abundance of cold temperatures. In fact, one of the bristlecones, the 4,700-year-old Methuselah, is the oldest-known continually growing living thing in the world. Some of these trees are so gnarled and barren of green that they seem almost like creatures with a multitude of arms turned heavenward (or, if you've seen *The Wizard of Oz* too many times, with arms about to reach down and snatch you).

Visiting this forest is completely worthwhile, but it's not a quick side trip. From Highway 395 in Big Pine, you have to drive thirteen miles on Highway 168 to White Mountain Road, then another ten miles to Schulman Grove, where the oldest trees live. The grove is above 10,000 feet, so the drive is a some-times-slow uphill climb (at least it's slow in my four-cylinder car). At Schulman there are two self-guided trails; the first is an easy one-mile stroll that takes you to the 4,000-year-old tree first discovered and dated by biologist Edmund Schulman. But try to allow time for the longer 4.5-mile loop trail into the Forest of the Ancients, where Methuselah is. That venerable tree is not marked, to prevent it from vandalism, so you'll have to try to guess which one it is.

If you can allow a whole day for this outing, and you have a car that can handle the rough dirt road, continue eleven miles past Schulman Grove to Pa-triarch Grove, which has some particularly beautiful bristlecones, including the largest ones in the world.

Bodie

Bodie State Historic Park

Hwy. 270 (between Bridgeport & Lee Vining), 13 miles east of Hwy. 395; or the southern route via unpaved Cottonwood Canyon Rd., reached by going 7 miles east on Hwy. 167 from Hwy. 395, just north of Lee Vining
(760) 647-6445

Open daily in summer 8 a.m.–7 p.m., in winter 8 a.m.–4 p.m.; snowmobiles, skis or s nowshoes may be required to reach the park in snow months; admission $3 per adult, $1 per extra passenger over 12

It's not easy to get to this remarkable ghost town, but the trip is part of the entirely worthwhile experience. In fact, if your car can handle it, I recommend taking the more challenging southern route, which requires driving eleven miles on a sometimes-rutted dirt road through a completely undeveloped high-desert landscape—it gives you a better idea of how profoundly isolat-ed and barren this once-booming Gold Rush town was. (Today, few take the southern route—most go the northern route, which requires only three miles of dirt-road driving.)

In 1859, '49er William Bodey grew tired of mining for too little gold on the other side of the Sierras, so for some bizarre reason he decided to prospect in this godforsaken part of the west, where the wind howls over hills of scrub and sagebrush. Unfortunately, he'd picked the coldest spot in the Lower 48—Bodie's summer temperatures are, on average, the nation's lowest (other than in Alaska), and in winter, it's not at all unusual to be 25 below zero—and he perished in the first winter, after staking a claim and finding just enough gold to attract a few other hopefuls. They kept mining for fifteen years after he died, with marginal results. Then one day in 1874, part of a mine collapsed and a huge vein of gold appeared. Before you could say "mother lode," the town of Bodie (the town founders changed the spelling from Bodey) had 10,000 souls. And most of them were not souls bound for heaven—at its peak, the town had 50 saloons and not a single church. Bodie became known as the wildest town in the wild, wild west, famed for gunfights, bar fights, prostitution, gambling and drinking.

The boom went bust in short order, with thousands of residents fleeing in search of other fortunes. Some hardy souls stayed on until 1932, but when a fire destroyed most of the residential areas, even they gave up. In 1962, the state took over the abandoned ruins, and ever since, park rangers, engineers and historians have made a tremendous effort to preserve Bodie in its state of arrested decay.

Although it looks large for a ghost town, what you see represents only five percent of what was once there—the fire of 1932 burned much of the town, and the elements took care of plenty more. But there's more than enough to explore. This is one of those rare historical sites that catches the fancy of almost everyone. Adults are fascinated by the stories in the self-guided tour booklet, in the film shown a few times a day in an old barn and in the books in the museum bookstore. And kids get a huge charge out of peeking in windows of the weathered houses, shops and businesses and seeing tons of artifacts, which are just lying around as if everyone fled the town in an instant. In one window we saw a child's bedroom, the wallpaper hanging off in decaying sheets, but a doll's stroller still sitting there. Dishes sit on kitchen tables, cans of food rest on kitchen shelves, coffins fill the old mortuary, and books lie on the schoolhouse's desks. Occupying the former miners' union hall, the museum is also filled with cool stuff, from the miners' ledger books, to children's toys, to clothing of the era.

Allow about an hour to drive to Bodie from Mammoth, perhaps a little more, and give yourself at least a couple of hours to explore the ghost town. Know that aside from a water fountain or two, there are no refreshments, so bring water and snacks or a picnic lunch, but take care not to leave any trash behind—the only trash here is from the 19th century. At this writing, summertime ranger-led activities included a history talk at 10 a.m., guided tours of the Standard Mill at 11 a.m. and 2 p.m., and regular showings of the film about Bodie history; times and events could change when you visit, however.

Finally, be warned that if you choose to attempt a visit between October and May, you could have snow on the dirt roads to contend with—and in the dead of winter, you might be able to get in only via cross-country skis or snow-shoes—just like the miners.

Devil's Postpile & Rainbow Falls

Devil's Postpile National Monument
Devil's Postpile Ranger Station
Minaret Rd., past Main Lodge, Mammoth
(760) 934-2289
www.nps.gov/depo

Open mid-June–mid-Oct., depending on snowpack

As is now the case at Yosemite, the flood of visitors and their cars got to be too much for the lovely San Joaquin River valley, where Devil's Postpile and Rainbow Falls are found. So now everyone except those camping in the valley must leave their cars at Mammoth's Main Lodge and take a shuttle bus down the narrow mountain road to these two natural landmarks. And when you see the summertime parade of buses, each one packed to the gills with people from all over America and the world, you'll understand why this rule came into being.

The main draw for these many visitors is Devil's Postpile, an extraordinary wall of columnar basalt, looking for all the world like towers of carved stone that were laid in place by skilled masons. Instead, this handiwork is credited to a volcanic eruption some 100,000 years ago. The basalt lava had an unusually consistent mineral composition, and it cooled unusually slowly, so when it contracted and cracked as part of the normal cooling process, these symmetrical towers were formed. Millennia later, a glacier came through the valley, carving away part of the formation and giving us the wonderful view of the Postpile that we have today.

The shuttle bus will drop you at the Devil's Postpile Ranger Station; from here, it's a short, easy hike to see the lava formations. Make the effort to hike to the top, where you'll see the glacially polished top of the Postpile, which looks like a custom-laid granite floor in someone's $100,000 kitchen remodel.

From Devil's Postpile, you can either take the marked 2.1-mile trail to Rainbow Falls or get back on the shuttle and ride one more stop, then take a 1.3-mile trail down to the falls. I recommend the former, which is quite a nice hike; the latter goes through forest that has not yet recovered from a fire a few years back.

If it's a sunny day, you really will see a rainbow—perhaps lots of rainbows—at Rainbow Falls, where a wide swath of the San Joaquin River's middle fork drops over a 101-foot cliff of volcanic rock. Some people go all the way down to the base of the falls, but I'd rather save my legs for the many other hikes in the area—you can see the rainbow just fine, and get a sense of the falls' power, from up high.

Inyo Craters

Inyo Craters
Inyo National Forest
Mammoth Scenic Loop, off Minaret Rd., Mammoth
(760) 924-5500 (Mammoth Ranger Station)

This part of the Eastern Sierra, from Mammoth to Mono Lake, is one of the youngest volcanic regions in the United States. In geologic time, volcanic explosions hit this forest just north of Mammoth Mountain a few seconds ago—but in human time, the explosions happened 600 years ago. Rising magma levels underground connected with groundwater, creating steam. This underground steam built to such an intensity that it finally exploded, blowing out rock, trees and earth to create three craters.

If you're in Mammoth in summer, it's well worth a quick outing to see the Inyo Craters. Found along the Mammoth Scenic Loop (a.k.a. the region's emergency-exit road in case of further volcanic or earthquake activity), the dirt road to reach them is marked with a large Forest Service sign. A short drive down the road will lead to a parking lot, and a quarter-mile walk through the woods will take you to two of the craters, whose lower basins are filled with water from rain and melted snow. (The third crater is atop Deer Mountain, a few hundred yards to the north.) The two craters are each about 600 feet across; the northern crater is about 100 feet deep, and the southern one is 200 feet. To stand on their rims and try to imagine the force of the explosions that made them—explosions from nothing more than hot water, mind you—is one of those "oh wow" experiences.

In winter, the dirt road becomes a terrific cross-country ski trail; this is a lovely time to visit the craters, when the forest is quiet and the massive pits are blanketed in snow. In summer, a fun, fairly easy ten-mile mountain bike trail winds through the crater area.

Mammoth Mine Ruins

Mammoth Mine Ruins
Various locations around Mammoth

California's gold fever wasn't limited to the '49ers of the western Sierra—Mammoth had its own gold rush, too. In 1877, a vein was discovered in Red Mountain (which really is red), and in no time, the population of Mammoth boomed from essentially zero to 1,500. The boom was much smaller and short-lived than in the western Sierra gold rush—it ended in just three years—but it seems to have been fun while it lasted. It had a second burst of energy in the 1890s, but that failed; in 1927, an entrepreneur named A. G. Mahan gave it another try, forming the Mammoth Consolidated Mine with his son, Arch, and tunneling into the side of Red Mountain. They pulled out some gold, but not enough to make it worth their while, so by 1933, that venture went kaput.

Today, ruins and relics from the various mine enterprises are found around Mammoth. My favorite mine ruins are what's left of Mammoth Consolidated Mines. To see these, drive through the Coldwater Campground at the end of Lake Mary. You'll see parking for the trailheads for Emerald Lake and Duck Pass; keep going to the next clump of parking spaces, and you'll see the entrance to the mine area. A lovely short stroll through flower-studded, pine-shaded forest will lead you to various bunkhouses, rusted equipment and a cool old log cabin that belonged to mine owner Mahan. When I was there recently, the cabin's rear windows had been unboarded, and we saw dishes still sitting on the kitchen table.

Also worth a peek is the Mammoth Museum, which is found on dirt Sherwin Creek Road just off Old Mammoth Road. (Open summers only; call 760-934-6918 for details.) This former log cabin houses a small but interesting collection of old photos, memorabilia and mining tools. It won't take long to view this collection, so afterward you'll have time to explore the ruins of the Mammoth Mine, which you'll find further along Old Mammoth Road on the way to Lake Mary Road. There's not much left—collapsed mine shafts, burned wood, an old concrete foundation—but after seeing the old photos in the museum, it's interesting to see what the area looks like today.

Mammoth Quake Fault

Mammoth Quake Fault
Inyo National Forest, off Minaret Rd., Mammoth
(760) 924-5500 (Mammoth Ranger Station)
Open outside of snow season for self-guided tours

Technically, this geological wonder is a fissure, not a fault—a fault is found in the plates under the earth's surface, and a fault moves side to side. Mammoth has a fault, to be sure, but it's underground and we can't see it. This amazing sight is a fissure, a huge crack in the rock and soil, most likely caused by a significant earthquake, although scientists aren't exactly sure what happened or when it happened. I'm just glad I wasn't in the neighborhood when it did happen.

From the parking lot, found just off Minaret Road en route to Main Lodge in Mammoth, you'll see various interpretive signs and a footpath leading through the quiet Jeffrey pine forest a short distance to the fissure. You can explore the massive crack from various places, but the most impressive is from the little bridge over a particularly rocky part. From here you can see how the two granite sides fit almost perfectly together, further proof that instead of being a side-to-side fault, this was a simple split that happened suddenly. The fissure goes down quite deep, perhaps 25 feet—far enough for bits of snow to still be on its floor, even in August. An impressive geological sight that is easily accessible (in the summertime) by anyone staying in the Mammoth area.

Manzanar

Manzanar National Historic Site
Hwy. 395, 5 miles south of Independence
(760) 878-2932
www.nps.gov/manz/expanded.htm

Open daily during daylight hours

A sad remnant of a sad chapter in modern American history—the internment of Japanese-American citizens during World War II—Manzanar is the best preserved of the ten former internment camps. Among the ruins on the 800-acre site are the sentry post, camp auditorium, lots of concrete foundations of former buildings and the camp cemetery. Many people take the three-mile self-guided tour by car, but the experience will be greatly enhanced if you take an hour or two to do it on foot. Then you'll get a more vivid sense of the isolation that must have been felt by the internees, as well as the natural beauty of the location, a typical Eastern Sierra desert overseen by magnificent mountains.

Allow some more time to explore the new Manzanar Interpretive Center in the restored auditorium. Besides the expected old photographs and mementos, the center has a creative collection of displays, including a guard tower, an accurately furnished replica of a barracks building, the barbed wire found around the perimeter, interactive exhibits that engage kids, and a short film produced by the National Park Service.

Two nearby venues also have museum-style exhibits that explain Manzanar's history, and both are well worth a stop. The first is found at the Eastern California Museum in nearby Independence (760-878-0258; open daily except Tuesdays and holidays 10 a.m. to 4 p.m.). The second is at the Interagency Visitor Center at the intersection of Highway 395 and Highway 136 in Lone Pine (760-876-6222; open daily 8 a.m.-4:50 p.m.).

Mono Lake

Mono Basin Scenic Area Visitor Center
Hwy. 395, 1/2 mile north of Lee Vining
(760) 873-2408
www.fs.fed.us/r5/inyo/vc/mono/
Open daily in summer; in winter on weekends; call for hours

First, let me save you a little embarrassment: It's pronounced "mow-no," not "maw-no." There—now you won't make the mistake I've made.

Mono is a lake like no other, a barren-seeming, much-evaporated body of water three times as salty as the Pacific ocean. It has no outlet, so once water gets in here, it stays, at least until it evaporates. Once fed by glaciers, Mono was, in its prime, some 600 feet higher; in the right light you can see the ancient watermarks in the nearby Sierras.

In 1941, the city of Los Angeles, thirsty for water beyond the huge amount it was taking from the Owens River, began diverting water from the tributaries that feed Mono, and over the next few decades, Mono's waters were increasingly taken. What was left became even saltier, too salty for some of the millions of birds that came here each year to feed, molt and rest on their annual migration. When the lake became threatened with extinction, biologists and environmentalists started screaming. The latter part of the 20th century saw Friends of Mono Lake work hard to achieve great success, saving the lake from extinction by forcing the DWP to stop further water diversion and help restore Mono's tributaries.

Today, the lake, its tributaries and its tufa towers are protected. The DWP still diverts water, but at a much slower pace and only if the lake's waters remain at a "safe" level. Only about 25,000 of the nearly one million ducks and geese who once visited annually still come—the lake remains too salty for most of them—but nearly one million other water birds (especially grebes and phalaropes) spend critical time here each summer and fall, and seagulls nest here each spring and early summer. The briny, salty waters of Mono are not hospitable to fish, but two creatures live here in abundance: minuscule brine shrimp and alkali flies, the pupae of which were an essential food for the local Paiute tribe.

What the lake is most famous for are its tufa towers, drippy stacks of calcium carbonate that formed underwater, back when lake levels were much higher. They look like something out of a Dr. Seuss book, beautiful in a strange, almost goofy kind of way. To get up close and personal with these tufa towers, head for the South Tufa Area, which is found on South Tufa Road, reached by driving several miles east on Highway 120 from Highway 395, on the lake's south shore. Nearby Navy Beach is the place to go if you want to try swimming in the lake, which you should—its salinity makes it amazingly buoyant. Just don't let your eyes get too wet, or they'll sting like hell.

Make sure to allow at least an hour or so for the superb visitor's center on a rise overlooking the southwest shore. (See also the listing on page 233.) It's really a small museum, with fascinating interactive displays on the natural history, geology and biology of Mono Lake.

Consider also experiencing Mono Lake from the water, especially in the early morning, when the water is still and the colors can be marvelous. The quietest way is to paddle a kayak next to a naturalist from Caldera Kayaks (760-935-4942, www.calderakayak.com). Or guide Tom Crowe will take you out in the early morning on a small, quiet motorized dinghy for a personalized tour; call (760) 647-6423.

Finally, if you are moved by the fragile beauty of Mono Lake and feel inspired to help it survive, contact the Mono Lake Committee, (760) 647-6595 or www.monolake.org.

Randsburg

Randsburg

Off lower Hwy. 395, about 20 miles south of Ridgecrest, or off Hwy. 14, via Redrock-Randsburg Rd. south of Red Rock State Park

(760) 374-2359 (museum)

Randsburg Museum open weekends & holidays (except Thanksgiving, Christmas & New Year's Day) 10 a.m.-5 p.m.; also open for groups by appt.

In 1895, so the story goes, three men saw gold lying on the ground, and before long this bit of nowheresville had more than 3,500 residents; at its peak, the Yellow Aster Mine, one of several here, had produced $25 million worth of gold. Today Randsburg has a population of 80, making it not so much a ghost town like Bodie (whose only residents are park rangers) but more of a faded Old West town. This desolate stretch of desert east of the southern Sierra range is actually home to a few almost-ghost towns, including Red Mountain and Johannesburg. But Randsburg is the most fun to visit, especially for kids, or if you're making that long drive from the Inland Empire to the Eastern Sierra and want a refueling stop with personality.

Randsburg may look like a ghost town, but the Rand mine operation is still employing local people and pulling gold out of the ground. Blazing hot in summer, freezing cold in winter and dusted with wildflowers in spring, this high-desert town has a few functioning businesses. Make sure to visit the general store, which has been operating continuously since 1896—it has pressed-tin ceilings, globe lights and a marble-countered soda fountain, where you can get a root beer float and a grilled cheese sandwich. Kids adore it. Across the street is the White Horse Saloon, which is usually open only on weekends, when ATV and motorcycle riders roar into Randsburg for lunch. It's known for hearty burgers and cold beer. Also open only on week-ends is the Randsburg Museum (156 Butte Avenue), a little house filled with memorabilia, a gem and mineral collection and displays of local history. And now there's even a surprisingly nice little B&B, the Cottage (760-374-2285, www.randsburg.com). A couple of quirky galleries and antique stores round out the commerce in town. Also worth seeing is the one-room City Jail (another favorite of kids), the restored abandoned barber shop, the adorable little church and the rusty mine ruins around town.

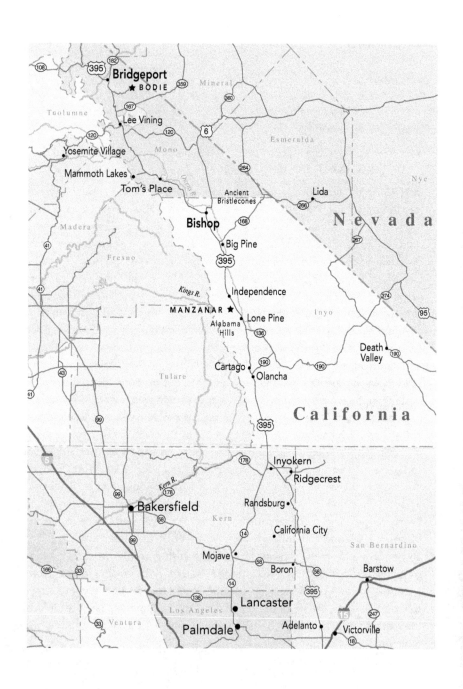

ROAD TRIP:
MAKING THE MOST OF THE 395 & 14

Henceforth I whimper no more, postpone no more,
need nothing,
Done with indoor complaints, libraries,
querulous criticisms,
Strong and content I travel the open road.
— Walt Whitman, *Song of the Open Road*

Here's where you'll find everything a road-tripper needs to know: Where to get the best coffee, what stops are worth making, where to find good grub or a good bed, how to avoid a speeding ticket, even who has the best restroom.

On the road
again

This chapter is full of finds for the traveler en route to the Eastern Sierra; most come from Southern California, although some take the northern route, via Bridgeport. This is not the only chapter, however, that includes places outside of Mammoth and June. Several of the sights in the "Top Ten Sights in the Eastern Sierra" chapter are found along Highway 395. Likewise, you'll find on-the-road places to fish in the "Gone Fishing" chapter, places to camp in the "Let's Go Camping" chapter, cabin resorts in the "Good Night's Sleep" chapter, and so forth.

How to **not** get a ticket...
and how to get there alive

Well, of course, the most obvious way is to follow the speed limit precisely, at all times.

Yeah, right.

Actually, some regular visitors and locals do just that. In fact, some of the most careful drivers on the 395 are the ones you'll later see barreling fearlessly down Climax. A fall on a snowboard is one thing, but a head-on collision with an SUV that's passing a truck outside of Olancha is an entirely different matter.

In the last couple of years, the California Highway Patrol presence has been significant on the 395 north of Olancha; on one trip I've seen as many as eight CHP cars writing tickets just between Lone Pine and Mammoth. They're not out there because they're bored. Highway 395, although much safer thanks to widening efforts, sees some horrible accidents. A friend who lived on the edge of Big Pine used to tell stories about lying in bed at night, listening to the tires squealing and metal crunching. Since 1997, 57 people have died on the 395.

After getting a couple of 395 speeding tickets and reading the accounts of the accidents, I've come to my senses. My family's quality of life did not deteriorate when our drive from Pasadena to Mammoth started taking five hours instead of four and a half. But that's not to say we go 60 miles per hour. Here are some thoughts:

→   **On Highway 14 between Palmdale and Mojave, and from Mojave to, say, Inyokern or Pearsonville, use your own judgment and follow the flow of traffic.** The CHP presence isn't strong in those regions, but they still show up. Some of these stretches are divided, proper freeways, which are much safer than two-lane highways. On some stretches, like where the speed limit is posted at 70 mph, 80 is doable.

→   **On the 395 between Pearsonville and Mammoth, or between Reno and Mammoth, don't go above 75 miles per hour (in the 65 mph zones).** Chances are you'll have plenty of cars blowing past you. The CHP is looking for them.

→   **When you pass through the towns, follow the speed limits assiduously.** If it says 25, go 25. For one thing, the sheriffs are lurking, but more importantly, these small towns have pedestrians, little kids, cyclists and all sorts of cross traffic, so it's just not safe to speed, even a little.

→   **Never pass at night.** A two-lane passing stretch is rarely more than ten miles away, and most of the time you only have to wait about five minutes. Visibility can be poor, and if a car coming the opposite way is going 90 (which happens a lot), you might not be able to get out of the way in time. Many of the worst accidents on the 395 involve passing attempts.

→   **Pass in the daytime only if you are absolutely, positively sure the coast is clear.** Again, cars coming from the opposite direction can be moving much faster than you think.

→   **If you're driving the lower 395, from Interstate 15 to Inyokern, make sure you've filled both the gas tank and the caffeine tank—it's a long, sleepy stretch with no signs of life except for the occasional Unabomber shack off in the distance.** Parts of this two-lane highway roll up and down, making visibility tricky, so be very careful passing, and don't pass at night.

→   **Finally, let the weather be your guide.** One of the great things about the 395 is that it is not a winding, treacherous mountain road, and most of it is usually snow-free. But if the rain's coming down hard, or it's snowing, or it's foggy, or the wind is howling, slow down—and turn on your headlights.

Best **coffee**

BISHOP

Kava Coffeehouse
206 N. Main St., Bishop
(760) 872-1010

Open Mon.–Thurs. 7 a.m.–8 p.m., Fri.–Sat. 7 a.m.–9:30 p.m., Sun. 7 a.m.–4 p.m.

A hangout for climbers and people with cool-looking dogs, Kava bills itself as "the finest Lithuanian coffeehouse in the Eastern Sierra," but they could leave out the word "Lithuanian" (owner Maria's ethnic heritage) and still be right. A rambling, colorful place with art for sale and vivid murals, it serves the excellent Alpen Sierra coffees and makes a perfect latte. There's a comfortable mix of tables and chairs, chess boards, a shaded sidewalk patio (for the dog people), several iMac computers with internet access, free WiFi for laptoppers, sandwiches, bagels, sweets, smoothies and some artsy gifts that Maria picks up on her world travels. All drinks are half price during the Friday happy hour, 5 to 6 p.m. Kava is one of my mandatory stops between Mammoth and L.A.

Spellbinder Books & Coffee
124 S. Main St., Bishop
(760) 873-4511

Open Mon.–Sat. 9 a.m.–6 p.m., Sun. 11 a.m.–4 p.m.

In the back of the bookstore is a coffeehouse with a few tables and the usual roster of lattes, mochas, espressos and drip coffees. A fine place to sip a cup while you start reading your newest book or magazine purchase. See also the review under *"Best Reasons to Stop,"* page 217.

MOJAVE

Primo's Coffee Bar & Grill
16862 Hwy. 14, Mojave
(661) 824-2012

Open Mon.–Thurs. 5 a.m.–10 p.m., Sat. 5 a.m.–11 p.m., Sun. 6 a.m.–10 p.m.

Unworthy of notice in any other burg, Primo's can be a godsend for drivers who just can't make it through Mojave without a shot of espresso. Their lattes and espressos won't put Starbucks out of business, but they're just fine. The food is standard diner greaseball fare

Best **food**

BIG PINE

Rossi's Steak & Spaghetti
100 N. Main St., Big Pine
(760) 938-2254

Open nightly 5:30–10 p.m.

The restaurant is fine, but those in the know head straight for the bar in this Big Pine steak joint—Russell, the bartender, serves up a fantastic tri-tip sandwich, the best sandwich on the 395. Russell grew up in the Owens Valley, and his family's been in the area since the late 1800s, so he has good stories, and you're likely to hear equally good stories from locals hanging out in the bar.

BISHOP

Amigos
285 N. Main St., Bishop
(760) 872-2189

Open daily 11 a.m.–9 p.m.

A good Mexican restaurant of the "Be careful, your plate is hot" variety, Amigos is also known for some unusually creative enchiladas, especially the tropical enchiladas Yucatan and enchiladas Autlan, stuffed with shredded beef, cheese and an avocado-tomatillo sauce, and topped with chipotle sauce. Amigo's is hugely popular with locals, so be prepared to wait for a table in one of the two cheerful, brightly lit rooms. Besides the enchiladas, the chile verde burrito and the tortilla soup are tasty.

Erick Schat's Bakkery
763 Main St., Bishop
(760) 873-7156

Open Sun.–Thurs. 6 a.m.–8 p.m., Fri.–Sat. 6 a.m.–9 p.m.

Personally, I don't get it. Sure the sheepherder and sourdough rye breads are tasty, and the deli counter makes a fine sandwich (the turkey is sliced to order), but why the mob of RVs, skiers and even tour buses? If it's not too crowded, this landmark place is well worth a stop for a sandwich, a cookie and a loaf or two of bread to take home (or eat in the car). But if the parking lot's packed and there's a crowd of people milling around the front, you might not want to wait 45 minutes. (If you continue south on the 395 to Lone Pine, you can get a sandwich made with Schat's bread at Lee's Frontier Chevron deli counter.)

Jack's Waffle Shop
437 N. Main St., Bishop
(760) 872-7671

Open daily 6 a.m.–9 p.m.

This large coffee shop has been a beloved stop for more than half a century. Good pancakes, eggs and, natch, waffles; the pies, cakes and cookies are also worth a stop. Evenings are popular with Bishop retirees having meatloaf, soup, pork chops and chili.

The Upper Crust Pizza Co.
1180 Main St., Bishop
(760) 872-8153

Open daily 11 a.m.–9 p.m.

A bright, cheerful place with both traditional pasta dishes and hip California-style pizzas, this place has become a Bishop success. Good pizzas include The Whites, topped with olive oil, fresh basil, garlic, tomato and feta, and Pearl's, with olive oil, basil, chicken, mushrooms and garlic. You can also get a classic pepperoni, or customize your pie. The salads are tasty, there's a good kids' menu, and you can sip a locally brewed beer or a decent glass of wine. It can get slammed on Friday nights as people head to the Sierras for the weekend, so you might have to wait awhile.

Whiskey Creek

524 N. Main St., Bishop

(760) 873-7174

Open Mon.–Fri. 11 a.m.–9 p.m., Sat. 8 a.m.–10 p.m., Sun. 8 a.m.–10 p.m.

Neither the food nor the setting are as appealing as at the Mammoth location, but the prices are lower and hey, there isn't a whole lot of competition in Bishop. The bar is relaxed and friendly, with captain's chairs, tall booths and a good bar menu; in between the bar and the slightly fancier restaurant is a gift shop of the potpourri-and-teddy-bear variety. The cooking is updated American, from burgers and grilled salmon to creative salads and Asian potstickers. A solid, reliable place filled with local rock climbers and on-the-road vacationers alike.

INDEPENDENCE

Still Life Café

135 S. Edwards (Hwy. 395), Independence

(760) 878-2555

www.stilllifecafe.com

Open Thurs.–Sat. 11 a.m.–2 p.m. and 5:30–9 p.m., Sun. 11 a.m.–9 p.m.

I cannot imagine anyone in their right mind driving through Independence and saying, "What this town needs is an authentic French bistro, and we're just the folks to do it!" But that's exactly what the French-Algerian family who owns this place said. So now, across from the Chevron and next to the tiny Independence Lions clubhouse is an honest-to-goodness French bistro, just like one you'd find in the 6th Arrondissement, or in SoHo or Santa Monica. This town doesn't even have a decent coffee shop! Outside of Olancha and Cartago, it's the deadest town on the 395—except inside the Still Life, which is packed on weekends (make sure to make reservations).

Anyway, the Still Life is not just an ordinary fish out of water—it's a damn tasty one. In a proper bistro room—high ceilings, French-mustard-yellow walls, white butcher paper atop white tablecloths, polished wood floors, old photos and California landscape paintings on the walls, a small bar—you'll be served onion soup, salade nicoise, steak frites, croque madames and all the French classics, prepared with good ingredients and plenty of skill. Don't miss the country pate, the garlicky escargots—they're excellent—the wild salmon grilled on the skin (served with braised leeks and mashed potatoes), the baby-greens salad with tomatoes, red onion, pine nuts and basil, and, for dessert, the tarte du jour. The few negatives are all understandable. I wish the service were a little brisker, but they do their best with a small staff (this is not the place for a quick road-trip refueling). I wish the napkins weren't cheap paper, given the higher-end nature of the place, but I'm sure there's no linen service in Independence. Hearty eaters find some dishes to be too skimpy, although personally I find them just right, in the French style. And the prices reflect the quality of the food, not the low overhead they must have in Independence.

All in all, Still Life is a wonderful incongruity, and it's a fine place for a leisurely French bistro dinner. Linger over the remnants of your wine (or Perrier, if you're driving) and listen to the remarkably good piano player. Who needs Paris? We've got Independence!

LEE VINING

Whoa Nellie Deli
Tioga Gas Mart and Mobil
Highways 395 and 120 West, Lee Vining
(760) 647-1088

See review under "Best Gas, Snack and Restrooms," page 211.

LONE PINE

Bonanza
104 N. Main St., Lone Pine
(760) 876-4768

Open Mon.–Fri. 11 a.m.–9 p.m., Sat.–Sun. 7 a.m.–9:30 p.m.

The best road food in Lone Pine—hell, probably the best Mexican food in the Eastern Sierra—is served inside a coffee-shop setting, in a place that was clearly once a cowboy-themed diner. Nowadays the Balderas family serves traditional Cal-Mex cooking: excellent fresh chips with homemade salsa, enchiladas stuffed with lean chicken and salsa verde, messy wet burritos, hearty, not-too-greasy carnitas and carne asada plates, Mexican beers...you know the drill. Though it hews to the beans-and-rice classics, the cooking is flavorful, and the ingredients are high in quality. For those who've just come off a backpacking trip out of Lone Pine and have been living on freeze-dried food, Bonanza is a dream come true.

Frosty Chalet

Hwy. 395, north end of Lone Pine
No phone

Open Mon. and Thurs.–Sat. 7 a.m.–7 p.m., Sun. 7 a.m.–3 p.m.

For some people (okay, for my kids), it isn't a road trip if it doesn't involve stopping for a soft-serve ice cream. And you won't find a better one in the Eastern Sierra. Not only does Frosty Chalet have the classic vanilla and chocolate, dipped or not, but it has all sorts of weird flavors (blue goo, coffee and cream) that kids love and parents find appalling. The fast food (corn dogs, burgers) is fine, too.

OLANCHA

Ranch House Café

Hwy. 395 , Olancha
(760) 764-2363

Open daily 6 a.m.–9 p.m.

Well located for road warriors who need a refueling stop between Southern California and Mammoth, the Ranch House has its fans and its foes. Some find the stuffed animals on the walls—including a huge moose head and a small black bear—to be creepy, and the breakfast is pretty weak. On the other hand, the knotty-pine booths are classics, and my kids are always happy with the grilled ham-and-cheese sandwiches, the crisp onion rings and the milkshakes. Stick to the simple stuff and don't order a hot sandwich unless you like a whole lotta gravy. There's a real espresso machine now, so you can get properly caffeinated for the road.

ROCK CREEK LAKE

Rock Creek Lakes Resort

Rock Creek Rd., 10 miles up from Tom's Place
(760) 935-4311

Open mid-May–mid. Oct. daily 7 a.m.–3 p.m.; general store serves soup, chili and pie (if there's any left) until 5 p.m.

Two Mennonite women, in white bonnets, floor-length print dresses and hiking boots, stopped in Rock Creek Lake's little café one morning, asking if they could pre-order (and pay for) some pie, so they could be guaranteed a reward after a long hike. "I'm so sorry," said resort owner and famous baker Sue King.

"We can't handle any pre-orders." The women looked crushed at first, then decided to cut their hike shorter so they'd be sure to get back before the pies were sold out.

Sue King's pie is that good. If Mennonite women can come from Pennsylvania to eat it, you can take a ten-mile (each way) detour off the 395 (up Rock Creek Road from Tom's Place) to have a piece of Dutch apple, lemon, peach or chocolate pie. Besides, you get to enjoy your pie in one of the prettiest settings in the west, on the shores of sparkling Rock Creek Lake, ten thousand feet into the High Sierra. Also worthwhile are the simple hot breakfasts, the three-bean turkey chili with excellent cornbread, and the homemade soups. The Kings are thinking of selling their place, which has regulars in a panic— let's just hope that Sue passes along her recipes and techniques if she decides to leave.

Best **gas, snack & restrooms**

ALL TOWNS

Chevron Gas Stations
Locations in Lone Pine, Independence, Big Pine, Mammoth, Mojave and Lee Vining

Chevron stations boast the cleanest gas-station bathrooms in California, so if you need a potty break, head for a Chevron. (Of course you pay for that cleanliness—the gas is often the most expensive.) There's a Chevron in every town from Mojave to Lee Vining; the lower 395 doesn't have a Chevron, or much of anything, so don't enter it with an empty tank or a full bladder.

INYOKERN

Brady's Mini Mart & Mobil

4467 N. Hwy. 395 (at Hwy. 14 junction), Inyokern
(760) 377-4733

Gas available 24 hours; store hours vary

The flip side of the hip Tioga Gas Mart, Brady's has to be the weirdest gas-station mini-mart in California. As a member of the Mammoth Forum once wrote, this place is so strange you almost expect the dwarf from Twin Peaks to be behind the counter. Sooner or later everyone stops here, either to fill their gas tanks or empty their bladders—it's the only sign of life at the juncture of the 395 and 14, and it's the last gas-and-pee for quite a while for southbound travelers. The gas pumps are modern, perfectly normal Mobil pumps—it isn't until you get inside and walk past the candy and chips toward the restrooms that you start to notice the bizarre stuff for sale: decks of Saddam Hussein cards, toy automatic weapons ("Hey son, let me buy you that AK47!"), crappy plastic tricycles, fart gum, tactical fighting knives (you never know when you might need one), a shockingly colorful plastic Jesus-on-the-cross lamp, Dale Earnhardt clocks, creepy stuffed animals that look like bad taxidermy, "collectible" figurines and, you guessed it, velvet paintings of dogs playing poker. You must to take some time to explore. The bathrooms are reasonably clean.

LEE VINING

Tioga Gas Mart/Whoa Nellie Deli

Hwy. 120, just above Hwy. 395 , Lee Vining
(760) 647-1088

Store and deli open late April–mid-Nov. daily 7 a.m.–10 p.m.; gas available 24 hours

Black-bean Southwest pizza at a Mobil station? Grilled salmon salad? Baja fish tacos? Welcome to the coolest gas station in the Eastern Sierra—hell, the coolest gas station in the country. You can fill up your car, get your fishing licenses and bait, pick up a fleece sweatshirt, power down a double-tall nonfat latte, send postcards to the gang at home, pick up all those camping essentials you forgot to buy at REI, and buy your kid a teddy bear, your mom an aromatherapy candle and your dad that Leatherman he's always wanted. Oh yeah, and you can eat chef Matt Toomey's amazing food. His Whoa Nellie Deli has to be the best gas-station deli in the world: eggs and bagels for breakfast, great sandwiches, a delicious barbecue potato salad, a superb Angus steer burger, mango margaritas, wonderful pizzas, lobster taquitos on a bed of delicious black beans, fantastic seasoned fries, bananas Foster…you'll never eat gas-station nachos again. The icing on the cake: The huge, grassy picnic area overlooks Mono Lake. Dinner can be memorable, as twilight changes the colors of Mono Lake and the stars start to pop out. If you call in advance, they'll have your food ready; great boxed lunches can also be prepared with advance notice.

LONE PINE

Lee's Frontier Chevron & Deli
1900 S. Main St., Lone Pine
(760) 876-4378

A better mini-mart than most, Lee's has a deli counter that makes tasty sandwiches with Schat's bread and good cold cuts; its chili-cheese fries and milkshakes are also popular with road-trippers. You can take your food to a table out on the porch, or head to the grassy area in back, where there's a picnic table under a big shade tree, with chickens poking around on the lawn. The bathrooms are good and clean.

Best motels
on the road

BISHOP

Best Western Creekside Inn
725 N. Main St., Bishop
(760) 872-3044, (800) 528-1234
www.bestwestern.com
Doubles $89-$189

The fanciest motel in Bishop, this is more like a hotel—for one thing, it doesn't have that insidious motel smell. Rooms are large and quiet, although the few facing Main Street (a.k.a. Highway 395) might be a little noisy, so ask to get one facing the sides or rear. The more expensive rooms overlook a pretty creek, with the Sierra beyond, but even the cheaper rooms have mountain views. And unlike some other chain motels in town, the air-conditioning system works well, the whole place is nonsmoking, and you can actually open a window (more precisely, a sliding door to a little balcony), so the rooms are free of that typical modern-motel stuffiness. On the downside, most rooms lack refrigerators and microwaves. But the free continental breakfast in the lobby is just fine. Fish cleaning is offered, even though this doesn't seem like a fish-cleaning kind of place. The pool and spa, set next to the creek, are the nicest in town. Families take note that a lovely little park, with a public pool and playground, is across the street.

The Elms Motel
233 E. Elm St., Bishop
(760) 873-8118, (800) 848-9226

Doubles in summer $50, in winter $45

If you need a cheap room in Bishop, you could do worse than the nineteen-room Elms. The location is quiet, off busy Main Street next to Bishop City Park, but it's also a short walk to restaurants and shops. Extras include fish-cleaning and fish-freezing facilities, an outdoor barbecue area and VCRs.

Joseph House Inn
376 W. Yaney St., Bishop
(760) 872-3389
www.josephhouseinn.com

Doubles $145–$165 summer, $130–$145 winter

Joseph House is not actually a motel, it's a B&B, and it's a mighty fine one. The location is bucolic, three acres alongside Bishop Creek, with a pond, weeping willows, rose gardens and arbors. The low-slung California ranch house has five bedrooms, each with private bath and each different from the rest; my favorite is the Garden Room, a bright room with comfortable seating but less fussiness than the typical B&B room. A lovely place run by a lovely family.

Mountain View Motel
730 W. Line St., Bishop
(760) 873-4242

Doubles in summer $67–$99, in winter $55–$99

This isn't a particularly attractive motel—it's your basic two-story stucco job with outdoor corridors. But it has a pool, which most non-chain motels in Bishop don't have, and its free continental breakfast is more generous than most. Some of the standard rooms have kitchens; families usually take the two one-bedroom suites with kitchens. There's also a good outdoor barbecue area with tables..

LONE PINE

Best Western Frontier Motel

1008 S. Main St., Lone Pine
(760) 876-5571, (800) 528-1234
www.bestwestern.com

Doubles $54–$93

A friendly motel of the low-slung, park-in-front-of-your-room variety, the Frontier is spotlessly clean. There's a little pool, a pet-friendly policy and country-cute pine furnishings in the rooms. The rooms set farthest back from the highway are, of course, the quietest, so request one of those.

The Dow Hotel and Dow Villa Motel

310 S. Main St., Lone Pine
(760) 876-5521, (800) 824-9317
www.dowvillamotel.com

Doubles $40–$55 in old hotel, $75–$115 in newer motel

The older part of this property, built in 1923, often housed movie crews shooting westerns in the nearby Alabama Hills; John Wayne was among the many cowboy stars who stayed here, and the place is practically a shrine to him, although Gene Autry and Roy Rogers also get their due. The bargain accommodations in the old building have old-world charm…and old-world rusticity, meaning the bathroom is likely to be down the hall, and the sound-proofing is nonexistent. But there's a comfy lobby with a big-screen TV and library of videos to watch, and the prices are hard to beat. Next door is the motel annex, which is less charming but has more modern comforts. There's a pool and spa.

Best reasons
to stop

In addition to the places below, see Chapter 10, "Top Ten Sights in the Eastern Sierra"—many of those destinations are found along the 395.

BISHOP

Mountain Light Gallery
Main St. at Line St., Bishop
(760) 873-7700
www.mountainlight.com

Open Sun.–Thurs. 10 a.m.–6 p.m., Fri.–Sat. 10 a.m.–9 p.m.

A beautiful showcase to Galen and Barbara Rowell, who died in a small-plane crash a couple of years ago, this gallery is Bishop's pride and joy. Galen Rowell was an acclaimed wilderness photographer who traveled the world and whose work often appeared in such publications as National Geographic; Barbara was a photographer of note, too, as well as a pilot. His great love was the Sierra, and collectors had prized his photos of the Eastern Sierra long before his death. Works from both Rowells are always on display, as are books from their publishing company, Mountain Light Press. Photography workshops are sometimes held.

Spellbinder Books & Coffee
124 S. Main St., Bishop
(760) 873-4511

Open Mon.–Sat. 9 a.m.–6 p.m., Sun. 11 a.m.–4 p.m.

If every small town in America had a bookstore like this, maybe we could solve all our problems. Readers hungry for good books drive from miles around to Spellbinder, which has been the best bookseller in the Eastern Sierra for 35 years. Located next to the Mountain Light Gallery, it packs a carefully chosen collection of 15,000 titles in a small space, with a particular emphasis on books about the natural world, including the Sierras; contemporary fiction, with discounts on all the Booksense bestsellers; travel; children's; and psychology/self-help. It also serves as a community center, where authors give talks and locals stop by to say hi to the owners. Check out the art cards by Bishop artist

Jill Kinmont Boothe, once considered the best woman skier in the world and the subject of the book and movie, *The Other Side of the Mountain*. In the back is a cheerful espresso bar.

Wilson's Eastside Sports

224 N. Main St., Bishop
(760) 873-7520
www.eastsidesports.com

Open Sun.–Thurs. 9 a.m.–6 p.m., Fri.–Sat. 9 a.m.–9 p.m.

Nirvana for mountain junkies, Wilson's is as good an outdoors store as exists. The focus is on camping, climbing and mountaineering, but you'll also find the best selection of women's activewear I've ever seen, as well as footwear for every mountain sport, telemark and snowshoe gear, guidebooks, topo maps and much more. Wilson's is also a great place to rent gear for Nordic and tele skis, snowshoes and camping and climbing gear; make sure to reserve rental gear in advance for busy seasons. The staff knows the Sierras as well as anyone, and they'll get you in the right gear.

INDEPENDENCE

Eastern California Museum

155 N. Grant St., Independence
(760) 878-0364

Open daily except Tues. 10 a.m.–4 p.m.; admission free

This fine little museum boasts a superb collection of basketry from two Owens Valley tribes, the Paiute and the Shoshone, as well as exhibits on local history. The museum is also known for its excellent exhibit, "The Story of Manzanar," which should be seen as a companion to visiting the nearby historic site (see page 198).

Mount Whitney Fish Hatchery

Off Hwy. 395, 2 miles north of Independence
(562) 590-5020 (DFG fish-stocking information)

Open Mon.–Fri. 7:30 a.m.–5 p.m., Sat.–Sun. 8 a.m.–5 p.m.

What a wonderful rest stop this makes! Just a couple of minutes off the 395, this outpost of the Department of Fish and Game is the largest hatchery in the state and the sole source of golden trout eggs in California. A fairly grand, 1916-vintage stone building, in which Fish & Game experts work to propagate baby trout, is fronted by a lovely trout pond surrounded by trees, lawns and picnic tables. This is a great place to stop for a picnic lunch on any Eastern Sierra road trip. If you have kids, bring a pile of quarters, so they can buy trout food from converted bubble-gum machines—the hefty fish go wild for the stuff. Most the stone building is off-limits to visitors, but there are good restroom facilities.

LEE VINING

Tioga Gas Mart/Whoa Nellie Deli

See review in "Best Gas, Snack and Restrooms," page 213.

LONE PINE

Diaz Lake

Hwy. 395, 2 miles south of Lone Pine
(760) 876-5656

On a hot summer drive along the 395, nothing is better than a jump in a lake—and right when you're about at your hottest, as you approach Lone Pine, you'll see pretty Diaz Lake, just begging to be jumped into. An 86-acre natural lake, Diaz has a small swimming beach, shady picnic areas, barbecue grills, restrooms and a pleasant campground. The water temperature is much warmer than at the higher-elevation lakes, so put on your suit and jump on in; a swim here is particularly heavenly if you've just come from a hike in the adjacent Alabama Hills. No boat rentals, so unless you brought your own, you won't be able to join the happy people out there waterskiing. But you can cast a fishing line from the shore—it is stocked with trout.

MOJAVE

Red Rock Canyon State Park

Hwy. 14 between Mojave & Inyokern
No phone

Visitor's Center open Sat. noon–8 p.m., Sun. 9 a.m.–3 p.m.

You always stop at Red Rock for a refreshing hike en route to the Eastern Sierra, don't you? Okay, me neither. But I always meant to, as I whizzed past the amazing displays of geologic history—huge plateaus of earth that were clearly forced upward from earthquake action that would have made the great San Francisco quake seem like nothing but a truck rumbling by. The reds, pinks and oranges of the earth and rock are gorgeous, the geology is dramatic… and yet we all speed by. So finally I stopped, went to the little visitor's center, got out of the damn car and went for a walk among the pinks and oranges and reds, and let me tell you, it's worth a stop. Slow down, stretch your legs, marvel and get yourself a little open-air geology lesson. At the visitor's center you'll find a map that will guide you to some good picnic-table spots.

MAPS

Maps encourage boldness. They're like cryptic love letters.
They make anything seem possible.
— Mark Jenkins, *To Timbuktu*

This short chapter will get you oriented: on the roads, the ski runs, the bike trails and the shuttle routes.

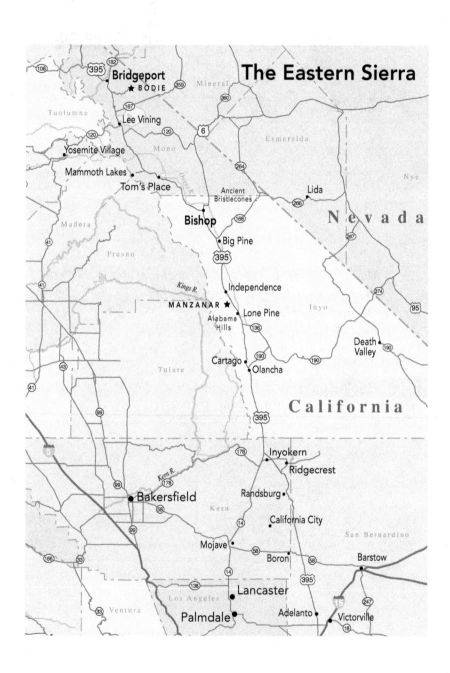

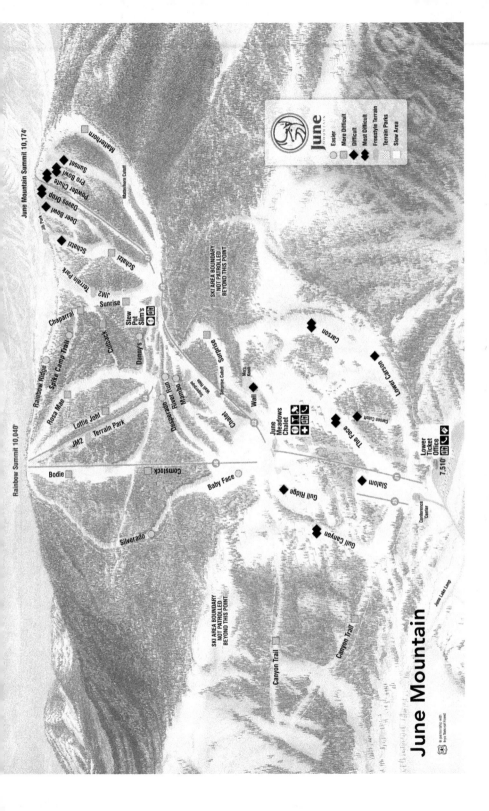

June Mountain

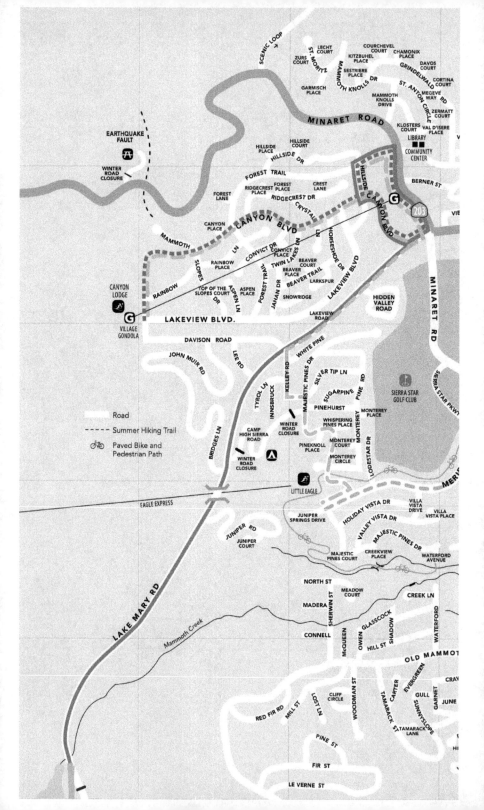

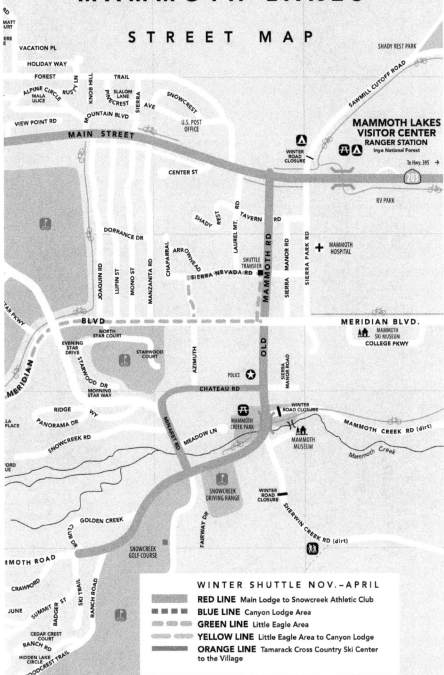

Mammoth Mountain

ESSENTIAL
RESOURCES

Learning keeps one from being led astray.
— Chinese proverb

This book is just the beginning. For more in-depth discussion and guidance on camping, fly-fishing, biking, the natural world and many other topics, see the recommended books, maps and websites that follow, and head for the region's fine visitor's centers.

Books

Best Easy Day Hikes: Southern Sierra, by Ron Adkison (Falcon, $6.95). This handy little pocket book directs readers to twenty fun hikes in the south part of the Sierra range; a little more than half are on the eastern side, from Olancha to Mammoth. Hikes range from just over a mile to an ambitious ten-mile day outing.

The Best in Tent Camping: Southern California, by Bill Mai (Menasha Ridge Press, $14.95). Subtitled "A Guide for Campers Who Hate RVs, Concrete Slabs and Loud Portable Stereos," this book is honest, inspiring and fun to read, and it's been a trusted resource for me. A number of Mai's favorite campsites are found in the Eastern Sierra.

Best Short Hikes in California's South Sierra, by Karen & Terry Whitehill & Paul Richins, Jr. (The Mountaineers Books, $15.95). You name the hike, it's in here, along with plenty of details on good campgrounds. The maps are clear, the descriptions are vivid, and the choices are many.

California's Eastern Sierra: A Visitor's Guide, by Sue Irwin (Cachuma Press, $18.95). This book is an absolute essential, the one book—besides this one, of course—that every visitor to the Eastern Sierra should have. Full of outstanding color photographs by such artists as the late Galen Rowell, as well as good maps, it is an engaging, thoroughly researched showcase of the region. You'll learn about the wildlife, native plants, geology, history, lakes, climate and sights to see. A labor of love by Irwin, worth far more than its $18.95 price tag.

Climbing Mt. Whitney, by Walt Wheelock and Wynne Benti (Spotted Dog Press, $8.95). If you hope to climb Whitney, pick up this book, which will guide you through the entire process. This is a not a hike to undertake casually, so read up!

Farewell to Manzanar, by Jeanne Wakatsuki Houston and James D. Houston (Bantam Books, $6.50). Reading this true story told by an American-born woman who was raised behind barbed wire in the Manzanar Relocation Camp will add a great deal of richness to your visit to Manzanar. This book is a staple in junior highs and high schools, particularly in California. Highly recommended.

Fly Fishing Mammoth, by Mark J. Heskett (Frank Amato, $9.95). The title says it all. Which flies work best on what streams and lakes, where the best spots are, advice on guides and the private fishing ranches in the region, and more information for diehard fisherman.

The Good, the Great, and the Awesome: The Top 40 High Sierra Rock Climbs, by Peter Croft (Maximus Press, $30). Serious rock climbers will find plenty of Eastern Sierra challenges in this well-regarded book.

Hot Springs of the Eastern Sierra, by George Williams III (Tree by the River Publishing, $10.95). This is kind of a goofy book, a poorly designed self-published little thing, but it is actually a terrific resource. Williams knows where every hot springs in the Eastern Sierra is hiding, and he gives away all the secrets in these pages. It's hard to find outside of Bishop and Mammoth, but you can order it on his web site, www.hotspringguides.com. A good investment for anyone who loves a long soak in a warm pool in the mountain air.

Mammoth Area Rock Climbs, by Marty Lewis (Maximum Press, $30). Rock climber, publisher and man-about-the-Eastern-Sierra Marty Lewis has produced the definitive guide to the many great climbs in and around Mammoth. The book isn't cheap, but it includes a wealth of detail, from topo maps to crag photos. See also his companion guides, Owens River Gorge Climbs and Bishop Area Rock Climbs.

Mammoth Lakes Sierra: A Handbook for Road and Trail, edited by Genny Smith (Genny Smith Books, $18.50). Genny Smith is the Naturalist Queen of the Eastern Sierra, having written about the natural history, geology and biology of the region for years. This classic field guide, first published in 1959 and now in its seventh edition, should be kept in the car for any 395 road trip and in the daypack for any hiking excursion. Curious about which mountain that is over there? Or what kind of flower that is? Or what that weird-looking rock is? Or what kind of trout that is in the creek? Or where a good hike in the area is? All those answers, and more, are in this authoritative book.

Mammoth: The Sierra Legend, by Martin Forstenzer (Mountain Sports Press, $49.95). The coffee-table book of the decade for Mammoth lovers, this weighty tome is a love song to the realizing of Dave McCoy's dream. Because it's published by the folks behind Ski and Skiing magazines, the emphasis is on skiing and other winter sports, although one gorgeous chapter is devoted to summer in Mammoth. The collection of photographs is dazzling, and the reading's good, too, especially when it focuses on the personalities, from McCoy himself to paraplegic ski legend Jill Kinmont Boothe to environmentalist, community leader and skiing Olympian Andrea Mead Lawrence. A terrific gift for anyone who skis or rides Mammoth Mountain.

Mountain Biking The Eastern Sierra's Best 100 Trails, by Reanne and Don Douglas and Mark Davis (Mountain Biking Press, $18.95). An impressive collection of mountain-bike trails throughout the Eastern Sierra, complete with detailed maps and photographs. A must for serious mountain bikers.

Sierra South, by Thomas Winnett, Jason Winnett, Kathy Morey and Lyn Haber (Wilderness Press, $17.95). Excellent maps and clearly detailed descriptions make this book essential for those heading out for backcountry adventures in the High Sierra. The book describes more than 100 back-packing routes, many of which are short enough to make for a wonderful day hike.

Water and Power, by William L. Kahrl (University of California Press, $24.95). Water and electricity might not seem like such an interesting topic, but then again, consider the greatness of the movie Chinatown. This acclaimed book tells the near-epic story of the battle for Owens Valley water, which began in the early 1900s and continues to this day. You won't look at dry Owens Lake the same way again.

Maps

Eastern High Sierra Recreation Topo Map (Fine Edge Productions, $8.95). Centered on the area from Crowley Lake to the south and Mono Lake to the north, this fine map is particularly suited to mountain bikers, because it details a wealth of bike-friendly trails. But it also has all the main hikers-only trails. four-wheel-drive trails and various hot springs and historic sights.

Eastern Sierra Guide Map (Automobile Club of Southern California, $3.95). This road map is particularly essential for campers—it gives details on every campground from Lone Pine to Bridgeport. It's also an accurate all-purpose road map, with details on the major sights and recreational activities in the region.

Mammoth Adventure Map (Sierra Maps, $8.95). Coated to handle repeated folding and unfolding, this highly detailed topographic map also has details on good hiking, cross-country skiing, equestrian, snowmobile and mountain biking trails, along with some basic travel information on sights, camping and transportation in the Mammoth area. Well worth keeping in your pack for hiking, biking and snow outings.

Mammoth Trails Hiking Trail Map (Eastern Sierra Interpretive Association, $5.95). Produced in association with Inyo National Forest, this is an easy-to-read topographic map containing descriptive text and map directions for fifteen of the most popular day hikes in the Mammoth area. The one map every day hiker should have.

Visitor's centers

Here are the various visitor's centers to help you better discover Mammoth and the Eastern Sierra. Hours and even locations may change (at least one center is building a new location), so call first.

Bishop Visitor's Center
690 N. Main St., Bishop
(760) 873-8405, (888) 395-3952
www.visitbishop.com

Open Mon.–Fri. 9 a.m.–4:30 p.m. (to 5 p.m. in summer), Sat.–Sun. 10 a.m.–4 p.m.

Located in the pretty city park, this all-purpose center is full of the usual brochures, souvenirs and maps, and you can get help finding lodging, campsites and information on activities. This is a good stopping area if you have kids, because the park has a fun playground, and there are ducks in the little creek.

InterAgency Visitor Center
Hwy. 395 at Hwy. 136, Lone Pine
(760) 876-6222

Open daily 8 a.m.–4:50 p.m.

Several public land agencies in the Eastern Sierra work together to run this visitor's center, which has a fine book and map store, displays on the history of Manzanar National Historic Site and a clear view of Mt. Whitney from its front porch. The people here can help with campground availability, news about weather and road conditions, and information on local sights, including the Alabama Hills and Owens Dry Lake.

Mammoth Lakes Visitor Center & Ranger Station
Hwy. 203 (Main St.), Mammoth
(760) 924-5500
www.fs.fed.us/r5/inyo/vc/mammoth.html

Open daily 9 a.m.–5 p.m.

This excellent visitor's center is an unusual joint venture of the town of Mammoth Lakes and Inyo National Forest, which has jurisdiction over Mammoth Mountain and much of the surrounding area. Its retail area has an outstanding collection of maps and books on the area, as well as a few choice T-shirts, posters and crafts and toys for kids. You'll also find free maps and brochures for area lodging, activities and restaurants, and a friendly person on duty who can help point you in the right direction. In summer there's a rich schedule of ranger talks, guided walks at places like Devil's Postpile, children's activities and campfire programs. A spiffy new visitor's center/ranger station is under construction and coming soon, not far from the old site.

Mono Basin Scenic Area Visitor Center

Hwy. 395, 1/2 mile north of Lee Vining
(760) 873-2408
www.fs.fed.us/r5/inyo/vc/mono

Open weekends in winter, daily in summer; call for hours

Located on the west shore of Mono Lake, this center is a must-visit to appreciate the area and its strange, salty inland sea. It's really more of a small museum of natural history than a visitor's center, with excellent exhibits on Mono Lake—you can study brine shrimp with a magnifying glass, guess your weight in brine shrimp, see how salty the lake is with a salt-shaker comparison, learn about Native American life at the lake, and feel different sorts of tufa. A screening room shows an interesting film on the lake throughout the day. Rangers are on hand to answer questions, and they give talks a couple of times a day. The store is one of the best in the region, with a superb collection of books and maps as well as fun stuff for kids. A fine example of our tax dollars at work.

Websites

Department of Fish & Game (DFG)

www.dfg.ca.gov/fishing

Come here to learn where to fish, information on fishing season, licenses and restrictions, and the latest news and fish-stocking reports.

Dr. Howard & the Dweebs

http://mammothweather.com

Mammoth real estate broker Howard Sheckter has won a loyal following for his weather site. The site is not just a promo for his services at Coldwell Banker—he really is a weather dweeb. The page contains all the current weather information, a web cam for people to check out the snow, plus long-range weather "discussions" (he stops short of calling them forecasts) that are followed with bated breath by many a skier. He's not always right, but his record is pretty good.

Eastern Sierra Fishing

www.easternsierrafishing.com

Michael Sommermeyer's site should be bookmarked by anyone who fishes the Eastern Sierra, or dreams of fishing there. He has up-to-date fishing reports from all the spots, from Bridgeport to Lone Pine; a few USGS maps of good lakes; a photo gallery; forums; feature stories on fishing; and some fish-stocking schedules (which could be more comprehensive).

GoMammoth

www.gomammoth.com

395.com

www.395.com

TheHighSierra

www.thehighsierra.com

These three linked sites are run by the same people. Because they are advertiser-supported, many of the links to, say, motels and outfitters are actually ads. But there's a wealth of fantastic information in these sites, from newspaper stories concerning the Sierras to CalTrans road information to details on backcountry skiing, horseback riding, camping, you name it. They can take some time to negotiate, but they're worth wandering around in.

Inyo National Forest

www.fs.fed.us/r5/inyo

This site has information on wilderness passes and permits, campgrounds, climbing Mt. Whitney, recreation opportunities and more. Its online bookstore has a fine selection of books and maps of the Eastern Sierra.

June Mountain

www.junemountain.com

All the basics on skiing June, including lodging information, weather, directions and prices.

Mammoth Forum

http://forums.mammothmountain.com

The online home for some of Mammoth's most dedicated skiers and boarders. People post all sorts of stuff here, from the snow levels on their front porches to requests for help in finding a good motel or restaurant. Many Forum regulars have become friends, and they post photos of their regular gatherings to ski, board, eat and drink together.

Mammoth Lakes Visitors Bureau

www.visitmammoth.com

A fine all-around resource for Mammoth, containing a broader range of information on activities, lodging, dining and transportation than the Mammoth Mountain site (see below), which is limited to Intrawest and official mountain activities and businesses.

Mammoth Mountain

www.mammoth-mtn.com

The lifeline for countless Mammoth junkies, this official Intrawest/Mammoth Mountain site contains everything from daily snow reports, to lodging information for Intrawest properties, to links to the best weather resources. The daily pictures are often terrific. Lots of information on Intrawest's summer activities, too.

The Mammoth Web Page

www.mammothweb.com

An all-purpose booster page that is advertiser supported. Good links for snow and fishing reports, road conditions (updated hourly) and activities. The restaurant page has handy links to menus, so you can get a good idea of what's to eat, but it seems like only paid advertisers get included.

National Weather Service

www.wrh.noaa.gov

From this main page, you can click to weather forecasts for Mammoth, Bishop and other parts of the Eastern Sierra.

Index